CHELTENHAM'S MUSIC

PETER GILL

SUTTON PUBLISHING

Sutton Publishing Limited
Phoenix Mill · Thrupp · Stroud
Gloucestershire · GL5 2BU

First published 2007

Title page photograph: The first publicity photograph of the Tilley twins, Peter and Paul. (*Anne & Jo Tilley*)

British Library Cataloguing in Publication Data
A catalogue record for this book is available from the British Library.

ISBN 978-07509-4617-9

Typeset in 10.5/13.5 Photina.
Typesetting and origination by
Sutton Publishing Limited.
Printed and bound in England.

*This book is dedicated to my son Ethan
for whom every note I sing is sung.*

Cheltenham Town Hall, *c.* 1950. The choirs are probably the combined forces of the Cheltenham Choral Society under the direction of Islwyn Jones (standing to the left of the mayor) and the Cheltenham Bach Choir – in those days the Bach choir occasionally augmented the Choral Society. The band is possibly the Cheltenham Silver Band and the general direction seems to come from Eric Woodward who is standing closest to the podium. Eric Woodward was an influential musical figure in Cheltenham for twenty-five years, most notably as conductor of the Cheltenham Philharmonic Orchestra and on occasion the Cheltenham Bach Choir. (*Anne & Jo Tilley*)

CONTENTS

To Jeanne,

With my very best wishes,

Vladimir Levinski (real name David Seccombe), the Cheltenham pianist who claimed to be the re-incarnation of Liszt. The tall, elegant Levinski, invariably dressed in Edwardian fashion, with a long black woollen overcoat, jackboots and sporting a monocle, was a familiar figure to Cheltonians in the 1950s. He was a brilliant, but temperamental pianist who regularly performed at the Cheltenham Town Hall for balls and on one occasion booked the venue for a magnificent performance which was only marred when halfway through the concert he became displeased, threw his music across the stage and stormed off. He later booked the Cheltenham Rotunda and afterwards the Winter Garden Pavilion at Malvern but then in 1952 his eccentricities brought him to the attention of the national press, whereupon he was booked to perform at the Wigmore Hall heralded as 'The Paganini of the Pianoforte'. The performance was a fiasco as he deviated from the published programme by playing Chopin's *Funeral March* and added passages to Beethoven's *Moonlight Sonata*, declaring himself 'the most controversial pianist of the century'. Clearly a disturbed man he died still in his thirties in the early 1960s in a residential home. *(Author)*

INTRODUCTION

Nestling in the heart of the Cotswolds, the Regency spa town of Cheltenham is probably not most noted for its musical achievements, the musical talent that has resided there or the musical bedrock that has underlain the town for at least the last hundred and fifty years. Cheltenham will probably be more quickly associated with National Hunt horseracing and the world-famous Cheltenham Festival held there each March. Some may associate the town with the 'spy-base' – the Government Communications Headquarters (GCHQ), with Regency buildings, in particular the Promenade, with the Literature Festival, the renowned public schools, Dean Close, the Ladies' College and indeed the (Gentlemen's) College, or simply its football team, which resides at Whaddon Road. Others may associate Cheltenham with one of the many notable persons who were born there, such as thirteen-times flat racing champion jockey Fred Archer who was born at 41 St George's Place in 1857, or Edward Wilson (who died with Scott in the Antarctic) who was born at 91 Montpellier Terrace in 1872, Arthur 'Bomber' Harris who was born at 3 Queens Parade in April 1892, or the actor Sir Ralph Richardson, who was born in 1902 at 11 Tivoli Road.

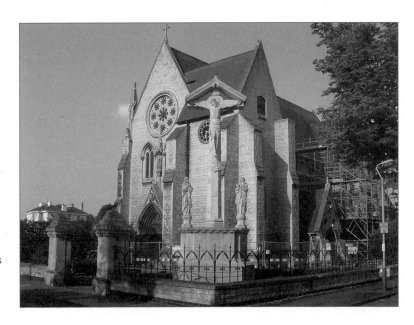

All Saints' Church where Gustav Holst's father Adolphus von Holst was organist. (*Author*)

No. 4 Clarence Parade (formerly
4 Pittville Terrace). This is the house in
which Gustav Holst was born on
21 September 1874 and is now home to
the Gustav Holst Birthplace Museum.
(*Author*)

If pressed as to what musical influence the town has or has had, it is possible that people will forget that it was here that Gustav Holst, composer of the *Planets Suite*, was born. Gustavus von Holst – he anglicised his name in later years – was born on 21 September 1874 at 4 Pittville Terrace (now 4 Clarence Road and home of the Holst Birthplace Museum), his father, Adolph von Holst, was the organist at All Saints' Church, an accomplished pianist who regularly gave recitals at the Assembly Rooms (a building demolished at the turn of the twentieth century which stood on the present site of Lloyds Bank on the corner of Rodney Road and the High Street) and conducted a chamber orchestra at The Rotunda (now also replaced by a Lloyds bank!). Between 1887 and 1891 Gustav was educated at Cheltenham Grammar School where his father also taught and upon leaving took up his first professional appointment as organist and choirmaster at St Laurence's Church, Wyck Rissington (about 10 miles to the east of Cheltenham), in 1892. While there he wrote the operetta *Lansdown Castle* (named after a tollgate on Gloucester Road), then in 1893 he moved to London to attend the Royal College of Music. The *Planets Suite*, for which he will always be best remembered, was composed during the tumultuous days of the First World War and given its first public hearing in September 1918 just two months before the Armistice. Holst returned to Cheltenham only occasionally, but most notably in 1927 when the town held a Holst Festival at the Town Hall at which was given the first performance of his recently completed work *Egdon Heath*. He died on 25 May 1934 aged just fifty-nine.

St Laurence's Church in Wyck Rissington where Gustav Holst had his first professional job, as organist and choirmaster aged seventeen. *(Author)*

The organ in St Laurence's Church today is the one that was played by Gustav Holst. *(Author)*

Marie Hall, the violinist for whom Vaughan Williams wrote and dedicated the work *The Lark Ascending. (Author)*

No. 9 Eldorado Road, the home of Marie Hall from 1911 until her death in 1956. *(Author)*

A classical artist working and performing at about the same time as Gustav Holst and receiving equal if not greater renown in her field was the violinist Marie Hall. Not generally remembered in the town, and certainly not widely associated with Cheltenham, Marie Hall was born in Newcastle on 8 April 1884 and received her first music lessons from her harpist father. In fact her first performances were made in the streets of Newcastle alongside her father. At the age of nine her talent was so obvious that she was accepted into the Royal Schools of Music in London where she had tuition from among others Edward Elgar. By the turn of the century her fame was already being established with tours of Europe and America. She gave her first public performance in Cheltenham in 1905 and went on to move to the town in 1911 when she married impresario Edward Baring, taking up residence at 9 Eldorado Road. Marie Hall was a violinist of quite exceptional talent and acclaim; indeed, such was her stature and the respect given to her by her peers that Vaughan Williams wrote and dedicated the work *The Lark Ascending* for her – of which she gave the first public performance in 1921. Marie Hall remained a resident of Cheltenham until her death in 1956.

Rosemead, 17 Eldorado Road, the first home of Brian Jones. *(Author)*

Of an entirely different musical nature to both Gustav Holst and Marie Hall (although he was also partly educated at the Grammar School) was the Rolling Stones founder Brian Jones who was born in Cheltenham (at the Park Nursing Home) in February 1942. Jones's first home was at Rosemead in Eldorado Road, and he was schooled locally at Dean Close between 1949 and 1953 and then at the grammar school from 1953 until 1959. He was by no means a popular figure among the teaching staff at the grammar school which was then under the headmastership of Arthur Bell; he was caned regularly and suspended on two occasions for his general disobedience and disdain of authority, which of course made him popular among his peers. He left the school and subsequently Cheltenham under a cloud when he was seventeen, having made his then fourteen-year-old girlfriend pregnant. For a while he travelled through northern Europe before returning to his home town for a brief spell, taking and losing a succession of jobs but playing in local bands at local venues. Even as a young boy he had shown great musical aptitude (helped by his pianist and choirmaster father) and in due course it would be said that he could pick up virtually any musical instrument and make it sing. Eventually Brian Jones decided to make his way to London to find his fortune. His love of jazz and blues and his

Brian Jones's headstone in Cheltenham Cemetery. The funeral of the founder of the Rolling Stones was held at St Mary's Parish Church in the town on 10 July 1969, seven days after the musician was found dead in his swimming pool at Cotchford Farm. *(Author)*

The 'Golden Boy' bust of Brian Jones that resides in the Beechwood Shopping Centre was designed and made by Maurice Juggins. *(Author)*

musicianship got him known to the right people in the right places and by early 1962 he had formed what was to become one of Britain's most successful bands, the Rolling Stones. Brian Jones died from drowning in the pool at his home, Cotchford Farm (once the home of A.A. Milne), in Sussex on 3 July 1969, less than a month after being sacked from the band that he had formed. He is buried at Cheltenham Cemetery in Prestbury.

Dame Felicity Lott was born in Cheltenham on 8 May 1947 – two years to the day after the end of the war in Europe. She started learning the piano when she was five, the violin at seven and then commenced singing lessons when she was twelve. She went to Pate's Grammar School for Girls, in Albert Road, and gave a small indication of what was to become when she appeared in school productions, for example *The Sorcerer* in 1962. She left Cheltenham to study French and Latin at Royal Holloway College, London, with the intention of becoming an interpreter, but music eventually controlled her destiny; in 1969 she returned to London to study at the Royal Academy of Music. Six years later she made her debut with the English National Opera in Mozart's *The Magic Flute*. Felicity Lott sang at the wedding of HRH Prince Andrew in 1986, was awarded the CBE in 1990 and made a Dame in 1996. She still maintains links with Cheltenham, performing regularly at the International Festival of Music.

Jeremy Coleman, better known as Jaz Coleman, is one of the most musically diverse musicians to have hailed from Cheltenham. Born there on 26 February 1960, his musical aptitude was in evidence at a very young age. From the age of six he learnt the piano and violin. He joined St Mary's church choir, Charlton Kings, and was later accepted to sing for the Addington Palace Choir in Surrey; as a consequence by the age of ten he had sung in many of England's great cathedrals and was given one of the greatest accolades a chorister can have, the St Nicholas Award. Within the next four years he had also won the Gold Cup at the Bath International Festival and the Rex Watson Cup at the Cheltenham Competitive Festival for his violin playing. However, all this would be a far cry from the music that would propel him to international fame and cult status. Jaz formed the post-punk band Killing Joke in 1979 with drummer Paul Ferguson. With their aggressive, almost violent performances and style they were founding fathers of the 'industrial' wave and would influence a generation of bands and musicians, including such heavyweights as Nirvana and Metallica. Killing Joke continue to record and perform all over the world but the influence that Jaz has is far more extensive. He has written and continues to write for films, and for orchestras of the stature of the New Zealand Symphony Orchestra and the Prague Symphony Orchestra, being composer-in-residence for the latter. In adulthood he has never stopped studying music and never stopped exploring and expanding the boundaries of musical genres, making him one of the most exciting and genuinely innovative composers working today.

There are other notable musicians who have had roots in Cheltenham at one time or another, such as Michael Burston, better known as Würzel, the guitarist from heavy rock band Motörhead, and Steve Ashley, the folk singer and songwriter who now lives in the town. He was an original member of the Albion Country Band and can boast Motown as the distributor and promoter on the other side of the Atlantic of two of his albums from the 1970s.

The Cheltenham Festival of Music was first held in June 1945 when the war in Europe had ended and the war against Japan was coming to a close, the dream of George Wilkinson, the then Cheltenham Corporations Entertainment Manager. It began with three concerts on consecutive nights at the Town Hall: Arthur Bliss, William Walton and Benjamin Britten all made appearances for the premieres of their most recent works. The success of the first festival ensured that the committee that Wilkinson had formed (consisting of Arthur Cole – the Musical Director, Cyril Hollingshead – editor of the *Gloucestershire Echo*, Eric Woodward – a piano salesman and amateur orchestra conductor, and Harold Chipp - a pharmacist with a love of music) would go on to organise another one the following year. In 2005 Cheltenham celebrated sixty years of the music festival.

More recently the town has promoted two other music festivals that have made an appreciable impact on the nation's cultural calendar. In 1996 the Cheltenham Jazz Festival first took place and the following year the Cheltenham

Folk Festival. Like their older sibling, these festivals attract some of the biggest names in their respective fields to perform in Cheltenham, and consequently entice music lovers into the town from outlying districts and neighbouring counties. Unfortunately, however, none of these festivals do a great deal for local talent as they look to promote established stars to fill the venues rather than looking on their own doorstep. This isn't to say that local musicians haven't benefited from the festivals. For many years during the Cheltenham Music Festival the council funded a Fringe Festival which highlighted local talent. It was an excellent opportunity for local musicians to reap the rewards of some general publicity and to perform for local people at no cost to the audience; but unfortunately council funding has now ceased. It must be said that an effort is still made by the organisers of the Jazz Festival to engage local musicians in a fringe festival, and long may it continue, but the impression remains that when finances are cut it is local musicians who are hardest hit.

Cheltenham is rich in public entertainment venues, some owned by the council, some privately owned. At one time local choirs, orchestras and amateur groups found it relatively easy and affordable to hire the Pittville Pump Room or the Town Hall for events. As I compiled this book it became evident that there is an overriding sense of regret, even bitterness, that the publicly owned venues are now not affordable for amateur musicians. As local choirs and orchestras are charged a similar rate to corporate clients it is inevitable that so many of their performances are now held in churches, church halls and even private dwellings rather than in the council-owned venues. It is generally feared that no local group will soon be able to afford to perform, even in the side rooms of the Town Hall or on afternoons at the Pump Room. However, there are still some venues that actively support local talent. The Playhouse Theatre is popular for amateur dramatics and the Bacon Theatre at Dean Close School actively encourages and assists local talent in filling its popular calendar of eclectic events. However, the gripe remains that, especially with the construction of the Centaur Suite at the Racecourse, which will inevitably take over as the venue for commercial touring concerts, the council should be encouraging use of its facilities by local groups.

This book does not focus on those who have achieved national and international fame, and it certainly doesn't herald the stars that have performed in Cheltenham at one time or another but other than that have little if anything to do with the town: it is well documented that the Beatles, the Rolling Stones, Jimi Hendrix and countless other sixties icons visited Cheltenham. Instead it aims to illustrate the fabulous musical foundations that were laid, created and are now maintained by the talent that has lived in the town. The real bedrock of Cheltenham's musical talent and status lies with the ordinary amateurs, semi-professionals and professionals who make up the choirs, orchestras, bands, rock groups, duos and soloists. To highlight any one individual would be disrespectful to so many others: perhaps the busker in the street on Saturday mornings has as much to offer as the conductor who leads the town's biggest orchestra, or the young group of teenage musicians performing in The Two Pigs, or the director of an amateur operatic performance at the Playhouse.

This book by no means shows everything that this town has had to offer, and there are gaping holes where I have not been able to illustrate a group or personality of particular influence. However, what I hope it does do is indicate the absolute wealth of ability, talent and commitment that has been in the town for well over a century.

This book is very much dedicated to those unsung (pardon the pun!) musical heroes as well as those who have been acclaimed. It is dedicated to every singer in every choir, every musician in every orchestra and band – anyone who has tried to enrich the lives of others by creating, however successfully or unsuccessfully, the food of love – music!

Peter Gill, April 2007

CHAPTER ONE

CHOIRS

The Bishops Cleeve Ladies' Choir who competed at the Cheltenham Competitive Festival of 1937. Back row, left to right: ? Willatts, Mary Rigby, ? Beard, Mary Cooper, Sam Stallard (accompanist), ? Kemble, Marjorie Tidmarsh, Molly Oldacre, ? Hobbs, -?-, -?-. Front row: ? Oldacre, Kath Hands, ? Hands, ? Stallard, E.E. Thomas (conductor), -?-, Alice Keen, ? Peacock, ? Denley. *(Cleeve Chorale)*

The members of the United Choirs of Cheltenham and district who gave a performance of *Merrie England* by Edward German in the Cheltenham Town Hall to raise funds for the Sportsman's Ambulance and Cheltenham Hospital Fund, 24 November 1940. The choir was under the direction of Islwyn Jones, and the orchestra that accompanied them was the Cheltenham Musical Guild Orchestra, conducted by Eric Woodward. *(John Keen)*

Cleeve Chorale, St Michael and All Angels' Church, Bishops Cleeve, 1991. Back row, left to right: Jean Bashem, Jill Latham, Diana Pratt, Margaret End, Judy Watkins, Ann Hookey, guest, John Phillips, Gerald Limb, Leslie Fulford, Lloyd Silverthorne (at the back), -?- (in front), Tom Forsyth, Julian Boyfield, Neilson Keyte, Ann Gedge, Joan Tebbutt, Richard Armitage, Mavis Tuffnell, Nigel Riley (accompanist), Hilary Swan. Front row: Margaret Riley, Joan Cawthron, Dorothy Brown, Sonia Kolaszynska, Judith Thomson, guest, guest, Brian Tebbutt, John Blenkinsopp (conductor), Brian Knight, Catherine ?, Karen Longmate, Marcelle Berry, Janice Plum, Sue Silverthorne. *(Cleeve Chorale)*

Above: Cleeve Chorale in the gardens of the Hellbrun Palace near Salzburg, May 2003. Their conductor is Iain Cooper who was appointed the previous September. Today the choir numbers about fifty members. The trip to Austria was their first foreign tour, but they followed it up in 2005 with a tour to Tuscany where they performed a memorial concert to Pope John Paul II in Florence. *(Cleeve Chorale)*

Choirmaster, organist, conductor and music teacher John Yarnley left a tangible hole in the Cheltenham music fabric when he died tragically in 2003. For many years he lived, quite appropriately, in a flat at 3 Queens Road which was also the Cheltenham exam centre for the Associated Board of the Royal Schools of Music for whom he was an examiner. He was at various times head of music both at Cleeve Comprehensive School and Pate's Grammar School where he had a huge influence on the musical ambitions of the students, encouraging all that showed interest, regardless of their ability. Among the many other musical positions he held in the town he was conductor of Cleeve Chorale for five years between 1979 and 1984, choirmaster and organist at St Mary's Church in Charlton Kings and an occasional musical director for local amateur groups, such as CODS (the Cheltenham Operatic and Dramatic Society) when they staged Gilbert and Sullivan's *The Gondoliers* in 1990. *(Simon Fletcher)*

The Cheltenham Grammar School Choir of 1946 was directed by the head of music Bill Neve, standing furthest left with the moustache. Next to him is another teacher, Mr Thomas. Roger Smith, who would become an influential figure in Cheltenham's music scene, is in the third row, fourteenth from the right. John Keen, the jazz trumpeter, is in the second row, eight from the right. Other identified faces include Don Biddle who is standing in the second row from the top, second from the left, Brian Fletcher is in the third row up, eighth from the right, Ron Farquharson is sitting furthest left beneath Bill Neve and ? Burch is sitting in the fourth row up, fourth from the right. *(John Keen)*

Cheltenham Bach Choir soloists at the Bach Festival, 1955. Left to right: Gordon Wallace-Hadrill, James Walkley, Maurice Hunt, John Poole, Marjorie Hyde, Eileen Hewinson, Barbara Dawson, Phyllis Adams. Cheltenham Bach Choir dates from 1946 when the dual energies of nineteen-year-old James Walkley and Ladies' College music teacher and organist of St Philips and St James' Church, Leckhampton, Sydney Shimmin, combined to create a choir originally dedicated to the music of J.S. Bach. *(Tony Whelpton)*

Cheltenham Bach Choir soloists and conductors following the choir's hundredth performance on 22 September 1959. Standing, left to right: Ralph Bailey, Myra Sanders, James Walkley, Diana Morris, Leslie Powell. Seated: Barbara Watts, John Poole, Phyllis Adams, Sydney Shimmin, Arthur Cole, Jean Mckinlay. *(Tony Whelpton)*

Cheltenham Bach Choir, 1954. The Bach Choir of today does not restrict itself by any means to the works of the baroque composer and several pieces have been written especially for it. It is widely regarded as one of the top amateur choirs in the south west and has over the years been associated with such musical luminaries as Dame Felicity Lott and Sarah Walker, who were both former members, and Brian Kay, founder member of the King's Singers, who conducted the choir from 1988 until 1998. *(Tony Whelpton)*

Cheltenham Bach Choir at the Town Hall in November 1960 with esteemed conductor Meredith Davies and the Birmingham Symphony Orchestra. As a replacement for Brian Kay the choir appointed Stephen Jackson as conductor and director of music in 1998. To act as his assistant they promoted Tim Morris (conductor of the Oriel Singers) from that of chorusmaster, a post he had held for nine years. *(Tony Whelpton)*

The Cheltenham Bach Choir at Pittville Pump Room with their conductor David Ponsford, 1986. As the reputation of the choir has grown it has enjoyed being invited to sing for such auspicious occasions as the BBC Proms, an Opera Gala in Birmingham Symphony Hall (with the Hallé Choir) and for the BBC's *Songs of Praise* in 2004. *(Tony Whelpton)*

The Smiths Industries Men's Choir, 1970. The conductor Dave Williams stands in the front in the centre; to the left of him is the choir's accompanist Mrs J. Gott. The choir dates back to May 1949 when a group of employees of Smiths Industries in Bishops Cleeve met one lunchtime to discuss the possibility of forming their own choir. Originally the choir was exclusive to Smiths' employees, but rapidly grew and in the course of time began to attract members from further afield. Until 1977 the choir was conducted by co-founder Dave Williams. It rehearsed weekly at the Labour Club in the Royal Crescent, Cheltenham. *(D. Baker)*

The Cotswold Male Voice Choir in rehearsal for a television appearance on HTV, 24 March 1976. They have appeared on television on two occasions, once on the dual quiz and talent show *Best in the West*, which their team won, and also on Hughie Green's *Opportunity Knocks* when they sang 'Standing on the Corner (watching all the girls go by)'. They were beaten in the show by Lena Zavaroni who went on to have her own television programme. *(Cotswold Male Voice Choir)*

The Cotswold Male Voice Choir in the Prince Michael Hall, Dean Close School, where they rehearse each Wednesday night. Centre in the light dinner jacket is Michael Power who has been musical director of the choir since December 2004. The accompanist is Geoffrey Mann, who also teaches the piano in Cheltenham. *(Cotswold Male Voice Choir)*

St Paul's Church Choir, *c.* 1950. Standing on the left in a dark gown is the verger Miss Herrington who was also a piano teacher. Standing together on the second row from the back, second and third from the left are Peter and Paul Tilley. Paul was head chorister and Peter was the church organist. *(Anne & Jo Tilley)*

Opposite: Leslie Burgess (light dinner jacket) is presented with a crystal bowl in recognition for his outstanding services to the Cotswold Male Voice Choir, 2001. The presentation by the chairman Bruce Rhodes (dark dinner jacket) was made following the choir's annual charity concert held at the Cheltenham Town Hall. Leslie was the musical director of the choir from 1977 until 2001. During this period he established a relationship with the Band and Trumpeters of the Life Guards which would see the choir and the Life Guards perform together at the Town Hall annually for sixteen years. Leslie has had a long and varied musical relationship with Cheltenham. During the fifties and early sixties he worked with local dance band leaders such as George Maisey, Bill Hartland and Peter and Paul Tilley. He gave Cheltenham conductor Roger Smith his first music lessons and then in 1965 went to St Paul's Training College in the town to become a teacher. In 1972 Leslie, who is also a skilled trumpeter, formed the Cheltenham Youth Brass for which he remained musical director until 1980 – passing the reins to Sue Mills who still holds the position. Leslie still augments local orchestras from time to time and is married to the accomplished soprano soloist Morfydd Burgess. *(Leslie Burgess)*

Cheltenham Spa Townswomen's Guild Choir in April 1955, showing off the Three Counties Federation Cup that they had won at Worcester earlier that month. Standing, left to right: Mrs Potts, Miss G. Hobbs, Miss L. Holman, Mrs M. Keeling, Mrs J. Weaver, Mrs J. Jones, Mrs S. Elliott, Mrs G. Watson, Miss M. Hogg, Mrs B. Hayward. Seated: Mrs E. Scott, Mrs F. Powers (pianist), Mrs Marion Keen (conductor), Mrs M. Doughty, Mrs S. Morrall. *(John Keen)*

Cheltenham Spa Townswomen's Guild Choir at the Brotherhood Hall, Charlton Kings, before a rehearsal, November 1968. Standing at the front, on the right, is the choir's conductor Marion Keen. *(John Keen)*

Charlton Kings Choral Society performing Mozart's *Requiem* at Charlton Kings Secondary School, spring 1965. Standing in the back row second from the right is long-serving member Peter Meason, now the choir's accompanist; the conductor is Kenneth Chatwood. The society was formed in 1957 through the combined energies of the vicar of St Mary's Church in Charlton Kings, the Revd Robert Deakin, Reginald Legg, the deputy headmaster at Charlton Kings Secondary School and also the organist and choirmaster at St Mary's, and Alfred Briggs, the headmaster of the secondary school. Reg Legg was installed as the choir's first conductor, seeing them through their first public performances which were mainly held in St Mary's Church. *(John Wright)*

Charlton Kings Choral Society annual dinner, February 1973. Nearest the camera is Ann Hookey; to her left are Mr and Mrs Hill. Along the back from left to right are Freda Martin, Brenda ?, -?-, Valerie Greet (sitting with her back to the wall), -?-, Mrs Deakin. Standing top right is the Revd R. Deakin, on his left is Doreen Munday and to his right is Laurence Hudson. At the main table, third in from the right, is Jeremy Spence. *(Ann Hookey)*

Marjorie Hooper and Alan Franklin, two of the founder members of the Charlton Kings Choral Society, photographed for the society's fortieth anniversary concert held at Pittville Pump Room on Saturday 29 November 1997. The fiftieth anniversary concert was held at Cheltenham Town Hall on 19 May 2007. *(John Wright)*

Charlton Kings Choral Society outside St Lawrence's Church in Bourton on the Water, early 1990s. *(John Wright)*

Charlton Kings Choral Society rehearses at Landolfshausen near Cheltenham's twin town of Göttingen in Germany, on a tour organised by George Compton in 1999. Conductor John Wright has been with the choir on all its European tours to date, which have included Brittany in 1995 and Scandinavia in 2002. In 2004 the choir gave the first public performance of John's own composition *In Praise of Earth's Beauty* at All Saints' Church in Cheltenham. John's wife Helen, who is a well-respected singing teacher, has also frequently performed solos with the choir. *(John Wright)*

The Gotherington Singers outside Cheltenham Town Hall, 1988. Standing left to right: Marie Bruce (accompanist), Dorothy Powell, Jenette Minett, Brenda Shelmerdine, Hazel ?, Lorna McMullen, Viv Hebdon, Lesley Nicholls, Helen Lammiman, Vi Wright, Marianne Heineman, Eugenie Clapham, Olive ?, Nig Tinkler. Kneeling: Margaret Crompton (conductor), Marian Wilson, Janet Hall, Shirley Hawey, Dawn Maisey, Mary Turner, Rosemary Thomson, Pat Peake, Barbara Murell, Barbara Shardlow, Elsie Hawker. *(Gotherington Singers)*

Opposite, top: Charlton Kings Choral Society, Pittville Pump Room, 2003. Standing in the centre is their conductor John Wright, who took over the reins from Kenneth Claxton in 1984. John left the area in 1987 and Ian Little became the choir's conductor until John's return in 1989. John studied at Trinity Hall, Cambridge, where he was an organ scholar and the Royal Academy of Music. He was for eight years the Assistant Director of Music at Cheltenham Ladies' College and today is a highly regarded piano teacher as well as being an examiner for the Associated Board of the Royal Schools of Music. *(John Wright)*

Opposite, bottom: The Gotherington Singers, 1986. Formed in 1967 as a small WI choir of between fifteen and twenty ladies in the village of Gotherington (just north of Cheltenham) by the present musical director and conductor Margaret Crompton, the choir has since built up a formidable reputation for its professionalism, style and dynamism and now has about forty singers. Weekly rehearsals alternate between Gotherington Village Hall and Bethesda Church Hall in Cheltenham. Regular tours abroad have included Malta, Spain, Jersey, Italy and Moravia. *(Gotherington Singers)*

The Gotherington Singers show off
some of their many trophies and
prizes. During their history they have
won the Folk Song Cup at the
Cheltenham Competitive Festival
(1995), the Gold Cup at the same
festival for the most memorable
performance in 2005, and on
27 April 1996 were Sainsburys'
Choir of the Day – heat winners of
the Choir of the Year competition.
Another prime concern of the choir
is their charity work – their concerts
and performances have raised
thousands of pounds for the British
Heart Foundation, James Hopkins
Trust, Winston's Wish and the
Samaritans, among other charities.
(Gotherington Singers)

The Oriel Singers standing on the pavement outside Cheltenham Town Hall, *c.* 1980. In 1975 four singers with Cheltenham Choral Society, George Mathers, Sue Chapple, Jennie Ursell and Ray Savery, decided to form a breakaway group to sing, for their own pleasure, a capella madrigals and motets which demand more discipline from the individual singer than larger choral works. They began to meet and rehearse on Sunday afternoons at the offices of architect George Mathers (fourth from the right) in Oriel Terrace, hence their name. In the autumn of 1975 they gave their first concert, conducted by Sue Chapple, to a Cotswold Women's Institute. By 1978 they had added a fifth voice, Pippa Holloway, and by 1979, with an influx of singers, it became evident that a director was needed. Tim Morris (tenth from the right) was approached to conduct and direct the singers. *(George Mathers)*

Opposite, top: St Andrew's Church, Montpellier, 10 December 2005. The Gotherington Singers stand with their patron and compère for the night Richard Baker OBE RD after their Christmas concert, which raised £2,382 for the Alice Glenister Trust. One of their soloists on the evening was Viv Nicholson who earlier in the year had won the Rose Bowl at the Cheltenham Competitive Festival. Also singing on the night were the Newhurst Singers, a smaller group made up of members of the Gotherington Singers. *(Gotherington Singers)*

Opposite, bottom: The Gotherington Singers meet Sophie, Countess of Wessex at St Martin in the Fields after singing as part of 'A Hallelujah for Dame Thora Hird', a memorial concert for one of Britain's best loved comediennes, 9 November 2005. As usual Margaret Crompton conducted the choir, Pauline Gearey was their accompanist and the soloists were Viv Nicholson and Dawn Maisey. The occasion raised over £15,000. *(Gotherington Singers)*

The Oriel Singers shortly after the choir was taken under the guiding musical wing of Tim Morris, *c.* 1980. Tim is standing second left at the back. Founder member George Mathers is standing at the back, furthest right, just visible. *(George Mathers)*

The Oriel Singers, *c.* 1993. Back row, left to right: Eric Axford, Paul Santer, Tim Morris, Damien ?, Phil Young, Jeremy Tyndall, Alasdair Jamieson, Alan Welchman, George Mathers. Front row: Dorothy Syster, Julia Morris, Janet Upton, Anna Jones, Rosy Jamieson, Mary Struthers, Christeen Ayton, Lindsay Tyndall, Palta Tolputt, Rosemary Nye, Jane Fitzgerald, Yoko Mathers. *(George Mathers)*

Above: The Oriel Singers, *c.* 2000. Under the leadership of Tim Morris the choir grew rapidly but numbers today are limited to twenty-eight voices. They give approximately twelve concerts a year to raise money for charity and their repertoire ranges from sacred to secular, serious to light-hearted. Tim, a sheep and arable farmer from Cirencester who is also chorus master of the Cheltenham Bach Choir, has guided the choir through many achievements, among them being finalists in the BBC Sainsbury's Choir of the Year in both 1986 and 1990, and BBC Radio 3 Choir of the Year in 2005. *(George Mathers)*

Since moving to Gloucestershire in 1983 Ian Higginson has made a significant impact on the musical life of Cheltenham. He is a well-respected organist, accompanist, conductor, composer, arranger and pianist. He is probably most recognised in the town as a conductor – he has been Cheltenham Choral Society's conductor since 1989 and the conductor of Jubilate Chamber Choir since its inception in 2001. He also teaches piano at St Edward's School. *(Ann Maltby)*

Probably Cheltenham's youngest chamber choir, Jubilate was formed in 2001 but that by no means undermines its quality. With conductor Ian Higginson at the helm Jubilate perform sacred and secular music from the last five centuries to an extraordinarily high standard and are quickly being recognised as Gloucestershire's leading chamber choir. Standing centre of the back row with a white bow tie is Ian Higginson.
(*Ann Maltby*)

Musica Vera at Cheltenham College Junior School, February 2005. Back row, left to right: Rick Benson-Bunch, Anthony Barlow, Ioan Davies, Mike Ellis, Tony Mason, Simon Graham, James Bryant, Peter Attwood, Rob Lygoe, Leslie Fulford, Peter Sands, Rab Butler, Lizzy Graham. Middle row: Julie Wand, Christine Reddaway, Nicola Ellis, Julia Magro, Catherine Lygoe, Sarah Rowbotham, Sarah Scull, Sue Guilford, Maddy Read. Front row: Angela Walker, Claire Alsop (conductor), Liz Ward, Sally Scanlon, Claire Read. Musica Vera (which translates as 'real music') was founded in 1964 by Graham Smallbone, director of music at Dean Close School, who remained as the choir's conductor until 1966. An early soloist in the choir was Felicity Lott who sang with them in Handel's *Messiah* on 13 March 1965 at Christ Church, when she was still at Pate's Grammar School. Today the choir performs three concerts a year, all held in Cheltenham, at which they raise considerable sums for local charities. *(Musica Vera)*

CHAPTER TWO

ORCHESTRAS

The Cheltenham Philharmonic Society at the Town Hall, Wednesday 19 February 1909. The conductor and prime mover behind the orchestra's formation was Charles Phillips. Just to the right of him are Finnish composer Jean Sibelius and the tenor John McCormack. This concert was a critical and financial success for the society. It opened with Wagner's *Meistersinger* overture, followed by McCormack's renditions of arias from *Lucia di Lammermoor* and *Carmen* and then Tchaikovsky's *Symphony no. 5*. Sibelius only took over the baton from Phillips for the orchestra to play *Valse Triste*, *Värsäng* and finally his own tone poem *Finlandia*. (*Cheltenham Philharmonic Society*)

W. Heller Nicholls, director of music at Dean Close School from 1894 to 1936, professional musician, composer of simplified piano music for young beginners and of the music for theatre productions including *The Secret Agent*, which was staged at the Cheltenham Opera House in 1911, produced by the CODS. An early and influential member of the Cheltenham Philharmonic Society, Heller Nicholls had associations with Brahms, Delius and Sibelius.
(*Cheltenham Philharmonic Society*)

In rehearsal at the Bayshill Lecture Hall is the Cheltenham Philharmonic Orchestra conducted by Eric Woodward. Eric's musical heritage was very impressive. His great-great-uncle Thomas Woodward had been organist at the parish church, St Mary's, in the centre of Cheltenham, while his grandfather had a musical instrument business in the Promenade; this was expanded by Eric's father, Albert, and moved to the High Street in the latter part of the nineteenth century. Albert Woodward was a talented violinist who played in the theatre orchestra. *(Cheltenham Philharmonic Society)*

The Cheltenham Philharmonic Orchestra performing at the Princess Hall, Cheltenham Ladies' College, under the guidance of their conductor Eric Woodward. By the 1930s the glory days of the Cheltenham Philharmonic Society had come to an end. With the country hit by hardship and depression this was very much the case for orchestras nationwide. Consequently the society joined forces with other local music societies to form a guild. The Second World War brought an influx of new talent into the town, largely displaced workers from London and of course service personnel, so in 1942 the society was able to regain its independence and was effectively reborn under the baton of Eric Woodward. He remained at the podium until 1955 when he emigrated to Canada. *(Cheltenham Philharmonic Society)*

Opposite, top: A presentation by Councillor T.L. Thompson, Cheltenham Mayor and president of the Cheltenham Philharmonic Society, to Eric Woodward on behalf of the society to mark the conductor's fiftieth birthday in 1952. The presentation was made at a reception in the Town Hall following a concert by the orchestra to mark both the conductor's birthday and the fiftieth anniversary of the laying of the Town Hall's foundation stone. *(Cheltenham Philharmonic Society)*

Opposite, bottom: To encourage new members to join its ranks throughout the 1950s the Cheltenham Philharmonic Society took an exhibition stand at the annual Cheltenham Hobbies Exhibition held at the Town Hall. This picture dates from 1956, the year that William Pritchard, Director of Music at Cheltenham College, took over the baton from Eric Woodward. *(Cheltenham Philharmonic Society)*

William Bell conducts the Cheltenham Philharmonic Orchestra in rehearsal. Bell was the conductor from 1968 until 1973, but he has remained very musically active and influential in the town ever since. Apart from acting as musical director for Cheltenham amateur dramatic and music groups, his most notable gift to the town was the formation in 1989 of Bel Canto Opera, for whom he was both the musical and artistic director. *(Cheltenham Philharmonic Society)*

Opposite, top: Cheltenham Philharmonic Orchestra rehearses Brahms's *Piano Concerto No. 1* in D minor in the Long Gallery, Cheltenham College, 27 March 1964. The orchestra's conductor is William Pritchard. At the piano is John Clegg and in the orchestra, in no particular order, are Leslie Burgess (trumpet), Jack Owen (violin), David Rust (violin), Ron Nourse (clarinet), Howard Vincent (clarinet), R. Fletcher (viola), John and Margo Jeens (cellos), Dr Hope Simpson (cello), Hilary Edwards (cello), David Twaites (violin), Bill Sutton (violin). *(Cheltenham Philharmonic Society)*

Opposite, bottom: Cheltenham Philharmonic Orchestra in rehearsal, 1966 or 1967. Pictured, but not listed in any particular order, are Tony Neville (flute), Liz Neville (oboe), Bob Eccles (bassoon), Howard Vincent (clarinet), Charles Vallance (clarinet), Duncan Westerman (oboe), Charles Smith (horn), Bill Simpson (flute), Pam Garratt Kerr (violin), Bill Sutton (violin), Mrs Tilley (violin). *(Cheltenham Philharmonic Society)*

Cheltenham Philharmonic Orchestra is conducted at the Town Hall by Duncan Westerman, June 1994. Duncan was the orchestra's ninth appointed conductor, having taken over from William Bell in 1973. He celebrated the centenary year of the ensemble in 1995 and in 2006 remains at the podium very much maintaining the traditions of his forebears, bringing music to Cheltenham that would otherwise not have been performed here. In recent years the orchestra has not just performed works by lesser known composers such as Julius Tausch, Spivakovsky and Paul Creston but also works by local composers such as Tony Hewitt-Jones, Philip Lane and Graham Whettam. They rehearse every Wednesday at St Peter's Church Hall, Tewkesbury Road, Cheltenham. *(Cheltenham Philharmonic Society)*

The Trumpet Fanfare for the opening of the Musicians' Ball at the Town Hall on 5 February 1952. On the front row furthest left is Paul Tilley. Ten years later Paul and his brother Peter's band were given the summer season at the Town Hall for the Saturday night dances. *(Anne & Jo Tilley)*

I. Braden conducts an eighty-five-piece band at the Town Hall, 5 February 1952. The occasion was the fifth annual Musicians' Ball held in aid of the Gloucester and Cheltenham Musicians' Union Benevolent Fund. During the evening 800 people were entertained by ten bands, which included the Al Kessel band, Arthur Cole and his Old-time Orchestra and Ken Lewty and his Orchestra. At the end of the evening, as seen here, all the bands came onto the main stage to perform five numbers. *(Anne & Jo Tilley)*

The Aircraft Components' Silver Band, led by Mr Gardner, 1938. This was essentially a works band for employees of Dowty's (George Dowty was the first president of the band) and would remain so until 1946, when a disagreement between George Dowty and the band over a playing commitment caused a rift that would result in the band largely disassociating itself from the company. It was renamed Cheltenham Spa Silver Band. *(Cheltenham Silver Band)*

Cheltenham Spa Silver Band having won the Fourth Section at the West of England qualifying contest in Bristol for the National Brass Band Championships, 1958. From this success the band was invited to play in the finals of the Fourth Section held in Hammersmith Hall, London, which they did on 25 October 1958, coming a very respectable sixth from twenty-one entrants. The following year the band won the Third Section of the West of England contest. Holding the cup in the picture is bandmaster Gil Gardner *(Cheltenham Silver Band)*

Cheltenham Silver Band after a period of turbulence, 1971. The 1960s wasn't an auspicious period for the band with many resignations of key members and a subsequent fall in numbers. With a few false dawns it wouldn't be until the beginning of the next decade that the band would really begin to increase in numbers again, largely through the influx of a group of children from Charlton Kings Junior School. *(Cheltenham Silver Band)*

Cheltenham Silver Band, with bandmaster Beryl Soul at centre front, 1995. The band gradually grew again in numbers during the seventies and eighties under a succession of bandmasters including the one-time Cheltenham Musicians' Union representative Ron Summers. In 1989 the band moved its rehearsal rooms from the Exmouth Arms on Bath Road to Ullenwood Court, where they still rehearse every Monday and Friday. *(Cheltenham Silver Band)*

Cheltenham Silver Band, 2005. The band is always looking for new members, but as can be seen here it has experienced an impressive regeneration since its worst days. Back row, left to right: John Hodges, Tim Kearsey, Matt Earl, Mandy Keedwell, Nicky Folland, Tom Folland, Nigel Hodges, Nigel Leach, Joyce Whiting, Nick Hallawell. Middle row: Chris Folland, Sheila Hudson, Eileen Morgan, Sophie Carpenter, Katherine Stanley, Jamie Kelly, Derek Walker, Beryl Soul. Front row: Rob Folland, Marcus Fisher, John Button (bandmaster), Sally Carpenter, Cindy Button. *(Cheltenham Silver Band)*

Cheltenham Chamber Orchestra before their concert at Pittville Pump Room, sometime in the 1990s. The dual conductors of the orchestra, Denise Ham and Robin Proctor, took over the position that Laurence Hudson had vacated in 1984 and worked in tandem until 2000. The orchestra was founded in 1968 by Laurence Hudson as an outlet for the talents of Cheltenham's professional musicians. *(Cheltenham Chamber Orchestra)*

Cheltenham Chamber Orchestra's woodwind section at Pittville Pump Room during the Cheltenham Festival in 1997. Back row, left to right: Helen French and Janet McKechnie (clarinets), Peter Kerr and Diana Lee (bassoons). Front row: Peter Tomlinson (flute), Janet Baldwin and Fiona Beck (oboes). *(Cheltenham Chamber Orchestra)*

Cheltenham Chamber Orchestra outside Pittville Pump Room following a rehearsal, 1990s. Dual conductors Robin Proctor and Denise Ham are in the foreground. The orchestra has established a reputation for performing music from the seventeenth century to the present day and regularly stages concerts at Pittville Pump Room and St Andrew's Church, Montpellier. *(Cheltenham Chamber Orchestra)*

Robin Proctor, the former conductor of the Cheltenham Chamber Orchestra who worked alongside Denise Ham between 1984 and 2000. Robin was also Director of Music at Cheltenham College in which capacity he conducted the college choir in major choral works at the Town Hall. He also accompanied the Cheltenham Bach Choir on the harpsichord in a performance of Handel's *Messiah*. *(Cheltenham Chamber Orchestra)*

Denise Ham, the former conductor of the Cheltenham Chamber Orchestra who worked alongside Robin Proctor from 1984 until 2000 and then upon Robin's retirement was appointed principal conductor until she stood down in September 2003. Denise is a gifted pianist and cellist and in the Cheltenham Arts Council Awards of 2003 she was a winner in the Instrumental Music Section, as well as being presented with the Joyner Cup for being the overall winner.
(Cheltenham Chamber Orchestra)

George Ewart, leader of the Cheltenham Chamber Orchestra since 2003. George has played with the English Chamber Orchestra, the Royal Opera House Orchestra, Covent Garden, and the English Symphony Orchestra.
(Cheltenham Chamber Orchestra)

Gavin Sutherland, current principal conductor of the Cheltenham Chamber Orchestra. Between September 2003 and January 2005 the orchestra was without a principal conductor, until Gavin's appointment. Gavin is a prolific and talented international musician, a pianist, composer and arranger, who first appeared with the CCO in December 2003, conducting the world premiere of his *Clarinet Concerto*. *(Cheltenham Chamber Orchestra)*

THREE

SHOWS

White Horse Inn staged at the Opera House by the Cheltenham Operatic and Dramatic Society (CODS) in 1958. Playing the role of the Emperor standing in the centre is Harry Gamble, to the right is Clive Young who played the head waiter Leopold and the girl directly to the right of Clive is Angela Simms who took the part of Josepha, the owner of the inn. *(David Palmer)*

The CODS production of *The Mikado*, staged at the new Everyman Theatre in 1960. When the Opera House closed in June 1959 the CODS were in danger of losing their spiritual home, for although their very first production in 1890 of *Trial by Jury* was held at the Assembly Rooms and their second production *Iolanthe* was staged at the Winter Gardens behind the Town Hall, since 1892 and their production of the *Pirates of Penzance* the CODS had held the majority of their shows at the Opera House, which was only opened in 1891. This is by no means coincidental as many of the directors of the new Opera House company were in fact members of CODS. In 1959 it was through the energies of, among others, many members of the society that enabled the old theatre to breathe new life, and indeed the debt owed to the amateur groups of Cheltenham should not be forgotten by current directors and managers of the Everyman Theatre. *(David Palmer)*

Opposite, top: The CODS production of *The Yeomen of the Guard* in 1964. The show was the seventy-fourth musical that the group had worked on since their formation in 1890 by Dr George Bagot Ferguson. Dr and Mrs Ferguson lived at Altidor in Pittville Gardens and it was there that many of the rehearsals for the first public production of the CODS were held. The production illustrated here was produced by D. Morris Hughes with the orchestra conducted and directed by John Gilbert. *(Jane Filby Johnson)*

Opposite, bottom: A publicity shot taken in Portsmouth for the CODS production in 1966 of *Hit the Deck* staged at the Everyman Theatre. Although a financial success this particular show was struck with a series of mishaps, including the last minute withdrawal of two Chinese actors who had been especially imported for the show, one of the main dancers pulling a muscle in dress rehearsal and subsequently missing the whole week of performances, and the non-arrival of wigs ordered from a firm in Manchester. *(Jane Filby Johnson)*

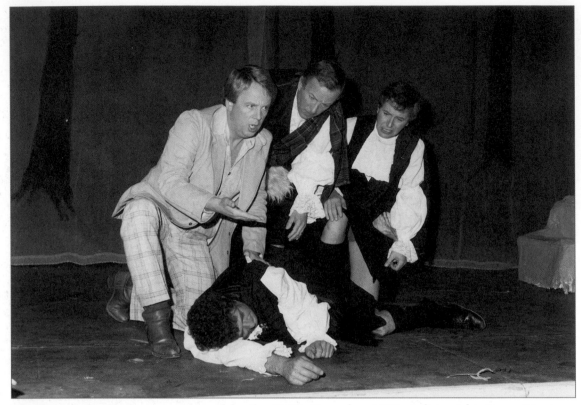

Brigadoon at the Playhouse, performed by the CODS, November 1983. Left to right: Bruce Morris as Tommy Allbright, Peter Wessen as Jeff Douglas, Geoff King as Charlie Cameron and on the floor Tony Maisey as Harry Ritchie. *(Jane Filby Johnson)*

Standing in the Playhouse foyer are Ron Knight (on the left) and Ron Turner. Both men were stalwart supporters of many of the amateur dramatic groups in the town, Ron Turner was from 1953 until 1962 the Hon. General Secretary of the CODS while Ron Knight assisted in many shows, frequently acted as a rehearsal drummer and played drums in other local amateur productions, including those put on by the Leckhampton Players. *(Jane Filby Johnson)*

The 1980 production of Rodgers and Hammerstein's *South Pacific* by the CODS at the Everyman. Angela Wright directed the show and conducting the orchestra was John Ursell, who would become head of music at Cleeve Comprehensive School. Pictured playing Stewpot is Alan Hall; to the left of him is Tony Maisey, who is talking to Sean Mayo, playing the role of Luther Billis. *(Jane Filby Johnson)*

Full-time musician Diggory Seacombe has acted as musical director for both Cheltenham's main amateur music and dramatic groups – the Cotswold Savoyards and the CODS, conducting the orchestras for most of the Gilbert and Sullivan repertoire as well as several other top musicals. He has also performed in the orchestra pit in his role as a percussionist. A man with many musical interests, he also teaches and has commissioned several new works for brass ensemble and percussion ensemble. *(Cotswold Savoyards)*

The Cotswold Savoyards' 1969 production of *Utopia Ltd* staged at the Playhouse – the company's eleventh production. The King of Utopia, with his back to the camera, is John Lynch. From left to right the men are John Blenkinsop, Roger Hill, David Johnson, Anthony Jones and John Hitchell. Standing to the right in the military uniform is David Manifold; Molly Barrett is just to the left of him. Conducting the orchestra is Michael Savage. *(Cotswold Savoyards)*

Opposite, top: The Cotswold Savoyards' very first production, *The Gondoliers*, staged at the Playhouse in October 1963. Centre stage are John Rattigan and Irene Leach playing the Duke and Duchess of Plaza-Toro respectively. The Duke is also holding the hand of his daughter Cassida, played by Beryl Rich. The company was formed by Paul Everington in 1962 specifically to produce the operas of Gilbert and Sullivan and the following year produced their first show. *(Cotswold Savoyards)*

Opposite, bottom: The Cotswold Savoyards' second production of *The Gondoliers*, this time put on in May 1970, again at the Playhouse. At the back of the stage are the Duke and Duchess of Plaza-Toro, this time played by David Churchill and Elsie Adamson respectively. The orchestra is being conducted by John Blenkinsopp, playing the oboe just in front of the stage and right of the violins is Duncan Westerman, while the two flautists by him are Lawrence Holloway and Harold Thomas. Wearing glasses and sitting to the right of the female clarinettist is Eric Phillips and furthest right, just visible playing the bassoon, is Bob Eccles. *(Cotswold Savoyards)*

The Cotswold Savoyards' 1984 production of *The Gipsy Baron* staged at the Playhouse. Conducting the orchestra is David Manifold, while in front of him just visible on oboes are Rosalind Honeywill and to the right of her Pamela Crompton. In the right-hand corner on bassoon is Jane Holmes. *(Cotswold Savoyards)*

The Cotswold Savoyards' production of *Iolanthe* staged at the Playhouse in 1985. The lead role was played by Ann Cox who can be seen as the fairy waving her wand in the centre. On the right of her is Neil Williams who played Strephon and next to him Howard Johnson who played the Lord Chancellor. The fifty-one-piece orchestra was directed by Diggory Seacombe. Peering up at the stage is Lucy Adams (flute) and two places to the right of her is Rosalind Honeywill (oboe). *(Cotswold Savoyards)*

Cotswold Savoyards' gentlemen of the cast for the 1986 production of *The Gondoliers*. Back row, left to right: David Manifold, David Johnson, Allan Gillespie. Front row: Douglas Brinklow, Neil Williams. *(Cotswold Savoyards)*

Cotswold Savoyards' ladies of the cast for the 1986 production of *The Gondoliers*. Back row, left to right: Josephine Llewellyn, Margaret Craven, Ann Cox. Front row: Christine Manifold, Barbara Fennell. *(Cotswold Savoyards)*

Cotswold Savoyards' ladies of the chorus for the 1986 production of *The Gondoliers*. *(Cotswold Savoyards)*

The chorus of the Cotswold Savoyards' 1991 presentation of Gilbert and Sullivan's *Utopia Ltd*. Back row, left to right: Ronald Behenna, Kate Badge, Ken Johnson, Jean Goldsbrough, John Pringle, Sharon Cogzell, Charles Davies. Middle row: Margot Sey, Julie Hiscock. Front row: Pat Manifold, Penny Lewis, Iris Holland, Pat Moulds, Moira Church. *(Cotswold Savoyards)*

The Cotswold Savoyards' 2004 production of Sondheim's *Sweeney Todd*. Shaving the man on the right and playing the role of Adolfo Pirelli is Paul Scott who also directed the production. *(Cotswold Savoyards)*

Opposite, top: The main cast of the Cotswold Savoyards' 1991 presentation of Gilbert and Sullivan's *Utopia Ltd*. Back row, left to right: Jim Abraham, Mike Bradley, Bernard Cox, Roger Badge, Raymond Kinghorn, David Manifold, Lionel Bassett. Middle row: Liz Llewellyn-Jones, Anthony Jones, Ann Cox, Euan Greig, Sim Small. Front row: Frances Hobbs, Christine Manifold, Helen Hooper. *(Cotswold Savoyards)*

Opposite, bottom: The Cotswold Savoyards' production of *Ruddigore*, staged at the Playhouse, November 2004. Centre stage is Karen Gillespie playing Mad Margaret and Paul Scott as Sir Despard Murgatroyd of Ruddigore – a wicked baronet! *(Cotswold Savoyards)*

The Cotswold Savoyards' production of *Sweeney Todd* in 2004. The music and lyrics are by Stephen Sondheim, indicating that the company no longer restricts itself to the musicals of Gilbert and Sullivan but produces occasional works by other composers and librettists. In recent years they have also put on

Offenbach's *Orpheus in the Underworld*, Bernstein's *Candide* and Reynolds and Slade's *Salad Days*. The musical director for this production was William Bell. *(Cotswold Savoyards)*

The Bishops Cleeve Choral and Dramatic Society with their production of *Café Continental*, March 1938. Back row, left to right: -?-, -?-, Catherine Oldacre, John Goss, -?-, ? Carver, ? Sayer, Jimmy Baylis, -?-, -?-, -?-. Front row: Edith Eager, Charlie Baylis, W Beard, -?-, -?-, -?-, -?-, Marjorie Goss, Mary Bowen, ? Linnett, Sybil ? , Amy ?, -?-, -? -, ? Peacock, Molly Oldacre, ? Denley, Mary Rigby.
(Cleeve Chorale)

Bishops Cleeve Choral and Dramatic Society production of Gilbert and Sullivan's *HMS Pinafore* in 1934. Back row, left to right: ? Boardman, ? Stallard, ? Stallard, ? Jones, Jim Baylis. Front row: Basil Gregory, ? Hobbs, Ralph Shipway, ? Moulton. The society was formed in the early 1930s, evolving from the informal meetings of a small group of singers in the village rectory. The society soon established itself in the village, staging regular shows and competing in the Cheltenham Competitive Festival. During the war the society was inactive and when it reformed in 1949 it was solely as a choral society. *(Cleeve Chorale)*

The production of *San Marino* by Bishops Cleeve Choral and Dramatic Society, 1939. Some of the people pictured are Catherine Oldacre (front row far left), Molly Oldacre (front row third from right) and Edith Eager (second row on the right). *(Cleeve Chorale)*

Opposite: Cheltenham's Sunbeams. During the First World War Mrs Winnie Townsend began to put on shows and concerts for the wounded troops billetted near her home in Stroud. Later she moved to Cheltenham where she became a dinner lady at Leckhampton Primary School and soon decided that she wanted to continue her productions for young people. She began inviting young girls to become 'Sunbeams'. A larger than life character, she choreographed her shows herself, accompanied the singing on the piano and made the costumes. Until the early 1960s she was organising the young female contingent of the town in shows and concerts. They would rehearse at Whaddon School and the Crown and Cushion pub on Bath Road and shows would be staged anywhere required, in hospitals, old people's homes or community centres, raising hundreds of pounds for charity in the process. This pantomime cast was photographed in the 1950s. *(Author)*

The Cheltenham Children's Theatre Association performing *The Wizard of Oz* at the Playhouse, 1986. The Cowardly Lion is Daniel Lloyd, Dorothy is Niki Danson, the Scarecrow is Bev ? and the Tin Man is Matthew Fisher. The Theatre Association put on its first production in 1958. All the shows were, on the whole, directed, produced, choreographed, musically directed and performed by eighteen-year-olds and under. *(Author)*

Niki Danson as Dorothy and Rachel Marland as the White Witch in *The Wizard of Oz*. The following year Niki would go on to direct the Children's Theatre production of *The Snow Queen* in which Rachel Marland would take the role of grandmother to Kay and Gerda. *(Author)*

In 1988 Cheltenham celebrated the bicentenary of the visit to the town of King George III, who spent a few weeks taking the spa waters in an attempt to cure him of what has since been largely accepted was porphyria. As part of these celebrations Leslie Burgess, who has a long musical association with the town and was also deputy headmaster at the time at Elmfield Junior School, wrote and staged a 'Cheltenham Celebration Concert' at Shaftesbury Hall Theatre on 9 May 1988. The show incorporated not just the musical talents of his own school, but also those of Leckhampton, Gloucester Road, Christchurch and Dunalley junior schools. Pictured above is Leslie addressing the audience beforethe concert began, with children from Leckhampton sitting behind him. *(Leslie Burgess)*

The young musical talents of Leckhampton Junior School Orchestra perform the overture to Leslie Burgess's 'Cheltenham Celebration Concert'. *(Leslie Burgess)*

Dorothy Frances in the lead role of Verdi's *La Traviata* at Didcot, 1975. Dorothy, who now lives and teaches in Bishops Cleeve, studied with Australian soprano Emelie Hooke who in turn had studied with Luisa Tetrazzini, the first along with Caruso to make recordings. Leaving music college in 1966, Dorothy was offered a contract to sing at Covent Garden where she would work with, among others, Joan Sutherland and Georg Solti, the latter of whom would recommend her for an Arts Council Scholarship. *(Dorothy Frances)*

Dorothy Frances established her Voice Studio in Cheltenham in September 1997, the same year in which she received the JPC 'Services to Music' award. Regardless of their ability she teaches all with the same enthusiasm and encourages all her pupils to perform in her annual charity fund-raising shows. The photograph shows 'The Boyfriend' number from 'Song through the Centuries'. Left to right: Kath Clayden, Michael Rowe, Martha Henry. *(Dorothy Frances)*

A dress rehearsal for the Dorothy Frances Voice Studio production 'Song through the Centuries' staged at the Bacon Theatre in 2001. This photo depicts the Madonna 'Who's that Girl' number with Sarah-Louise Browne taking centre stage. On the left of Sarah is Yeu Hung Quach and on the right is Stuart Foster. Each year Dorothy offers a scholarship to her pupils, awarded on the basis of achievement or potential. Sarah-Louise was the first recipient of this scholarship. *(Dorothy Frances)*

Mezzo-soprano and Cheltenham hairdresser Cathy Keating, who along with competing successfully at the Cheltenham Competitive Festival (in 2003 she won the mezzo-soprano class) and appearing on stage with several amateur dramatic companies, regularly produces and stages her very popular 'Music to Delight' concerts, which are held at the Prince Michael Hall at Dean Close School. *(Author)*

William Bell during a rehearsal for his last production with Bel Canto Opera in February 2007. A Cheltenham musical establishment in his own right, William Bell has been part of the town's music scene since 1967 conducting, among others, the Cheltenham Philharmonic Orchestra and the Cheltenham Opera Group. He founded Bel Canto Opera in 1989 to present fully produced operas with orchestras at venues throughout Gloucestershire. In 2006 he conducted Bel Canto in a brilliant, mammoth concert version of Verdi's *Aïda* at the Pump Room in Cheltenham. *(William Bell)*

A rehearsal scene from *The Magic Flute* in 2007, the last production of Bel Canto Opera. The productions combined the most talented singers and orchestral players from Gloucestershire and Worcestershire, with the principal roles being taken by professional singers. The productions were always ambitious and widely acclaimed and were sung in English: from 1996 Tom Boyd, the stage director, wrote new versions of the libretto especially for the company. Left to right: Alexander Anderson-Hall, who played the part of Tamino, Susan Black, Maria Jagusz and Eamonn Dougan, who played Papageno. In 2006 the Cheltenham Arts Council awarded Susan Black the Joyner Cup for her services to music. *(William Bell)*

FOUR

POST-WAR
MUSICIANS

The Blue Rhythm Band of St Paul's Youth Club at a dance held at St Paul's Church Hall in aid of the Cheltenham Sea Cadets, October 1949. It was the first gig for the band, who were all members of the club. Playing accordion on the left is Cyril Skeen, Paul Tilley is playing trumpet, while directly behind him is the drummer Mike Davies, Peter Tilley is playing saxophone and directly to the left of him, slightly turned, is the pianist Ernest Cooper. Standing front right wearing a tie is John Little, then an apprentice french polisher at Ernest Trapp. *(Anne & Jo Tilley)*

Opposite, top: Peter Tilley and his Music, *c.* 1951, pictured in one of the many venues in which they regularly played for dances. From the end of the war until the beginning of the 1960s Cheltenham had several popular show or dance bands who would perform at dances in and around the town in village, church and community halls. Probably the most popular band of the period was that of Al Kessel, who kept performing right up until the 1980s, closely followed by Harry Lang's Showband, and then from the early 1950s Peter Tilley with his twin Paul established their outfit on the scene. Left to right: Roger Mansell, Paul Tilley, Peter Tilley, Ernest Cooper. *(Anne & Jo Tilley)*

Opposite, bottom: The first appearance of Peter Tilley and his Band (note the name change) at Cheltenham Town Hall on the occasion of the fifth Annual Musicians' Ball, 5 February 1952. Cyril Skeen is on piano, A. Davis on stand up bass, and fifteen-year-old Norman Nichols on drums; in front are Peter Tilley on tenor saxophone, D. Newman on alto saxophone and Paul Tilley on trumpet. Shortly after this the brothers were called up for National Service, first being sent to Innsworth where they were asked to form a camp dance band and later to Hereford, where they put together the first military band for the base. *(Anne & Jo Tilley)*

The Casey Court Skiffle Group at The Wesley Hall in St George's Street, 1956. Left to right: Tony Holbrook, Robert Shaw, Colin Boulton, Peter 'Buck' Jones , Colin Hyde, Graham 'Nod' Stodart. The band originally formed in 1955 under the name of The Worried Men, changed to Casey Court in 1956 and the following year, as personnel changed, became The Ramrods. *(Graham Stodart)*

Opposite, top: The Peter Tilley Dance Band at Gloucester's Guildhall, 1957. Pete is in the white dinner jacket playing tenor saxophone and twin brother Paul is at the back on the right playing trumpet. Returning from National Service the twins soon re-established themselves in the area, not just with their big band, which held residencies at the Chase Hotel in Ross-on-Wye, the Marine Ballroom in Evesham, the Guildhall in Gloucester and Cheltenham's Town Hall, but also for their many other entrepreneurial activities, most memorable of which were their chimney sweeping business and their hair salon named 'Paul et Pierre'. Competing with the other local big bands of the time run by Bill Hartland and Trevor Brookes, the Tilleys used a five on three line up (five saxes with a three-piece rhythm section of piano, bass and drums – plus a trumpet) to perform the big band sounds of Neil Hefti, Glenn Miller and Nelson Riddle. *(Anne & Jo Tilley)*

Opposite, bottom: The Dowty Resident Dance Band, early 1950s. The Dowty Social Club put on dances each week for the employees and their families for whom this band would perform. There is no longer a resident band but the Dowty Social Club still regularly books both local and not so local musicians to perform for their members. *(Author)*

The Ramrods at the US Airforce Base at Fairford. Left to right: Ken Matthews (manager), Graham Stodart, Tony Holbrook, Peter Jones (at the drums), Phil Crowther and John Davies. The late 1950s and early 1960s were a golden time for the band; they frequently supported big stars at the Town Hall such as The Shadows, Joe Brown and Johnny Kidd and the Pirates. For a brief period in 1961 Brian Jones, who would go on to form the Rolling Stones, joined the band playing saxophone. For a while the band had to change their name to Phil and the Ramrods after the chart success of an American band with the same name. Then in 1963, as bookings began to arrive from further afield, the commitment of being in a band began to tell. Graham was the first to leave, in October 1963, and tragedy struck when singer and guitarist Phil Crowther died on his honeymoon the following year. Within eighteen months the band had finished. *(Graham Stodart)*

Opposite, top: The Basement Jazzband playing in the Filbys' basement, 38 Priory Street, *c.* 1958. Originally just a rehearsal area for friends of Mrs Filby's son Guy to play jazz, the basement of 38 Priory Street soon became the 'in place' for Cheltenham's youth and the original 'jamming' trad jazzers led by John Picton soon became the house band. In this permutation of the Basement Jazzband are, from left to right, Bernie ? (clarinet), John Lewis (bass), Roddy Snell (trumpet), Dilly Bedwell (drums), John Keen (valve trombone), -?- (banjo). *(Jane Filby Johnson)*

Opposite, bottom: The Delta Jazzmen, one of the many Cheltenham jazz bands that benefited from the experience of performing in the basement of 38 Priory Street, *c.* 1959. Left to right: Harry 'Squeak' Brampton (clarinet), John Lewis (bass), Bill Nile (trumpet), Pete Sumner (banjo), Tat Meager (drums) and 'Bif' (Adrian Montague-) Smith (trombone). *(Jane Filby Johnson)*

The Young Socialists' float for the Battle of Britain parade in Cheltenham, 15 September 1962. Left to right: Dave Butler (drums), Alan Carter (banjo), Dick 'Duck' Pond (bass), Mac White – later of the Temperance Seven (clarinet), John Keen (cornet), Graham Ride (alto saxophone). *(John Keen)*

Opposite, top: The Delta Jazzmen, who were later known as Bill Nile's Delta Jazz Band, were a popular Cheltenham band who regularly pulled the crowds into dances at the Rotunda in Cheltenham and for all-night raves at the nearby Cranham Woods right until the mid-1960s. Then the entire band moved to the greener grass of London where they rented and moved into a house in Muswell Hill – wives, girlfriends, children and all! At about the same time the band changed its name once more to that of the Bill Nile Goodtime Band. Left to right: 'Squeak' Brampton, John Lewis, Bill Nile, Tat Meager, Pete Sumner, Bif Smith. *(Jane Filby Johnson)*

Opposite, bottom: John Keen playing the valve trombone with his band in the early 1960s. Between 1960 and 1962 John employed Brian Jones in his band to play guitar, purchasing for his use a Vox AC15 amplifier from Ray Electrical in the Lower High Street. With the jazz scene dying almost overnight with the emergence of the Beatles, John left Cheltenham in the mid-1960s to go to London where he continued to play, while also working as a teacher and later as an educational psychologist. John returned to Cheltenham in later years but continues to regularly play in London where he has performed with Chris Barber and leads the hugely popular West London Rhythm Kings. *(John Keen)*

The Jaguars and their proud fathers at The Hay Lodge in Newnham, *c*. 1962. Left to right: Bill Lee, Geoff Peacey, Rick Tirley, Roger James, Peter Lee, Rob Peacey and Jack Peacey. A popular and successful young teenage band, The Jaguars worked throughout the Forest of Dean and into Gloucester and Cheltenham, metamorphosing into The Advocates. All the band members were skilled musicians and would individually move on to play in many different bands locally, nationally and internationally. *(Peter Lee)*

The King Bees, *c.* 1964. This was a rhythm and blues band from Cheltenham which had a markedly different sound to the regular guitar-based bands of the day by including Ritchie Brookes on Hohner Pianette. They played the usual pub and dance venues of the time, such as St Mark's Community Centre, St Luke's Church Hall and of course the Town Hall, where they supported among others Alexis Korner and Alex Harvey. Left to right: Paul Mason (bass and vocals), Ritchie Brookes (electric piano and harmonica), John Eyles (lead guitar), John Maisey (vocals and harmonica), Paul Cook (drums). *(R. Brook)*

Opposite, bottom: The Advocates, *c.* 1963. Left to right: Rob Peacey, Graeme Brown, Peter Lee, Roger James and Geoff Peacey. A typical teenage band of the Beatlemania period, The Advocates would later become The Good Goods after some personnel changes. Of particular interest is Rob Peacey, playing guitar, who is now much more familiar to Cheltenham audiences as a saxophonist, and his brother Geoff, better known for his keyboard skills. Geoff Peacey went on to work with The Solents (who later became Mott The Hoople) and Boston (who later became The Gary Glitter Band); he currently works in Germany for CBS. Graeme Brown would go on to play in Pendulum, along with such local names as Paul Holder, and John Beckingham and Roger James played in Buster James and Crow. *(Peter Lee)*

The Alley Cats in a local skittle alley, 1964. Left to right: Andy McTaggart (lead singer and harmonica), Dennis Carpenter (bass guitar), Dave Ralph (rhythm guitar), Ricky Aulsebrook (lead guitar) and Dave Townsend (drummer). Originally The Alley Cats were called Vince and the Vigilantes. When their lead singer Vince returned to his native Ireland they brought in Andy McTaggart as his replacement. For a while the group kept the same name, but as Andy became more embarrassed about being called Vince and getting tired of wearing the previous singer's huge white stage coat, they decided to change their name to The Alley Cats. Managed by Mr M.J.D. Henderson, they were one of Cheltenham's most organised young bands of the sixties. As well as owning their own equipment and having stage costume they recorded a demo disc of two original tracks – a rhythm and blues song entitled 'Keep Still Baby' on the 'A' side and a ballad 'Be Mine' on the 'B' side, which was subsequently played by none other than Jimmy Saville on his radio show. The group also had their own fan club run by Susan Vizor and Sue Watt. *(Andy McTaggart)*

The Dedicated Soul Band, *c.* 1966. Four of the band were originally members of the King Bees who decided to move on from rhythm and blues into soul after supporting Zoot Money. They brought in the saxophones of Colin Brook and Pete Best, changed their name and learnt a different set. Left to right: Colin Brook (saxophone), Pete Best (saxophone), Paul Mason (bass and vocals), Ritchie Brookes (electric piano and harmonica), Paul Cook (drums), John Maisey (vocals, harmonica and trumpet). *(R. Brook)*

The Dedicated Soul Band (also known as the Dedicated Soul Set), *c.* 1967. Hailing from Cheltenham, they claimed to be the Midlands' first big soul band. Back row, left to right: Colin Brook, Ritchie Brookes, Pete Best. Front row: Paul Mason, John Maisey, Paul Cook. *(R. Brook)*

Ameba Triad, *c.* 1968. A popular Cheltenham band who went on to feature and win their heat on Hughie Green's *Opportunity Knocks* under the name of Whitcombe Fair. Left to right: Roy Perkins, Ernie Redding, Ritchie Brookes, Keith Viner. *(R. Brook)*

Andy McTaggart, former lead singer of The Alley Cats, here singing with the Sack o' Woe at RAF Innsworth, 1969. The band actually called themselves A.M. James with the Sound of the Sack o' Woe, with Andy taking the alias of A.M. James. It wasn't the first and wouldn't be the last time that he used a stage name in his musical career. The saxophone in the background is being played by Colin Gibbons. *(Andy McTaggart)*

FIVE

THE 1970s
& 1980s

The John McKinlay Sound, *c.* 1970. One of Cheltenham's popular show bands of the early 1970s, they were often booked for dinner dances at such venues as the Queen's Hotel. Left to right: John McKinley, Chris Gregory, Ritchie Brookes and Paul Holder. *(R. Brook)*

A 'pick-up' jazz band passing the Queen's Hotel during the Battle of Britain Carnival. The trombonist at the front on the left is Peter Holmes, the one on the right and facially obscured is Warren Short; on the bass drum behind is Pete Barnard. *(John Keen)*

The Paul Dean Band performing at the Town Hall, mid-1970s. The Tilley brothers split their resources and pretty much monopolised the live bookings engaged by the Town Hall by offering two separate bands, the Peter Tilley Band and the Paul Dean Band. If a bigger band was required they would pool their resources. Paul Tilley, wearing a suit, leads the band; behind him on organ is Bob Holland. *(Anne & Jo Tilley)*

Decameron, the highly successful folk-rock band of the early 1970s, *c.* 1974. Decameron were formed in 1968 by two songwriters, Johnny Coppin and Dick Bell, who were both students at Cheltenham Art College. Soon they enlisted another friend and guitarist Al Fenn, then cellist Geoff March, and under the management of one Jasper Carrott they began to play the folk clubs. In 1973 they released their first album, *Say Hello to the Band*, on Vertigo Records, following which bassist Dik Cadbury joined the band. Three other albums were to follow, the third one of which, *Third Light*, came out on Transatlantic Records in 1975. The following year the band broke up. Johnny Coppin was the only member to continue as a full-time professional musician, although all kept performing in one way or another and occasionally the band reforms for reunion concerts. Left to right: Al Fenn, Geoff March, Dik Cadbury, Dave Bell, Johnny Coppin. *(Dik Cadbury)*

Opposite, top: Carol & the Clubmen, one of the very typical small combos on the Tilley Brothers' books, performed all over the Cheltenham region. The 1970s began to see a sharp decline in work for live bands as mobile discos put their feet in the door. However, agencies such as those run by the Tilleys and Norman Brodie of the Gloucester Entertainment Agency still offered bands regular gigs at local clubs such as Walls, ICI and Dowtys as well as occasional dinner and dances in local hotels. Appearing here with Carol is drummer Geoff Hawker who has remained a popular and respected drummer on the local music scene to the present day. *(Anne & Jo Tilley)*

Opposite, bottom: The pre-punk, progressive rock band Chylde, *c.* 1973. It featured the electric fiddle of Martin Mitchell, Bob Williams on bass, Neil Webster on lead guitar and Alleyn Menzies on drums. Chylde were extremely popular among Cheltenham's student fraternity and were frequent performers at the Pavilion Club (pictured), situated in Montpellier Gardens by the tennis courts and now demolished, and The Stable at the Plough Hotel, now the site of the Regent Arcade. *(Alleyn Menzies)*

Folk-rock band Madrigal in a publicity shot, 1975. Left to right: Martin Mitchell (electric violin and recorder), Alleyn Menzies (drums), Tony Bennett (lead guitar and flute) and Steve Hutt (bass guitar and mandolin). Madrigal were formed in 1974 by Steve Hutt, Richard Amey, Martin Thomas and Martin Bennett, inspired by the music of French electric folk player Alan Stivell. Within a year Martin Thomas and Richard Amey had left to be replaced by Alleyn Menzies and Martin Mitchell. At just twenty years of age Steve Hutt showed considerable entrepreneurial skills managing his own and other bands through the Supernova Entertainment Agency. He also organised the Sunday evening folk club at the Carlton Hotel. *(Steve Hutt)*

Bob Holland playing guitar for the Peter Tilley Band, 1977. Bob had a long association with the Tilley brothers, beginning in April 1971 when he joined Paul's band (the Paul Dean Band) as guitarist. Shortly afterwards the organist, Dick Bell, left and Bob began filling in on organ as well. Bob continued to work with Paul until 1976 while also playing with other local bands such as Colours, which consisted of Carlos Alvarez, David Curran, Peter Hedworth (who went under the stage name Peter Lee), Steve Moth and John Davis. In 1978 Bob started working with the Peter Tilley Band and remained with him until 1983. Other bands that Bob played with around this time were The Sundowners featuring Irish button accordion player Pat Carr, Pat Daly and Jimmy 'Mack' and The Chicago 7. From 1978 Bob also started playing solo gigs on the piano – starting at Creepers in Cambray Place, on the baby grand piano in the basement. Bob is today recognised as a jazz pianist of consummate skill. *(Anne & Jo Tilley)*

At Cheltenham Town Hall for an Arts Ball are, from left to right:, Peter Tilley (saxophone), Stan Lowe (drums) and Peter Hedworth (singer). Peter Hedworth was a popular big band singer who often featured with the Crescendo Big Band but was known more familiarly by his stage name of Peter Lee. (*Anne & Jo Tilley*)

Ritchie Brookes in a publicity pose from the late 1970s. Ritchie was taught the piano classically by two of Cheltenham's better known teachers, Mrs Martin from Whaddon and Dorothea Reynolds from Pilford Avenue in Leckhampton, the latter renowned for having had one of her arms amputated in a rail accident. Throughout the sixties and seventies he was in a succession of bands which included the King Bees, Dedicated Soul Set, Armageddon, The Mondays, Ameba Triad, The Junkyard Angels, Joint Dream, The John McKinlay Sound and Jason's Flock, many of whom were Cheltenham-based, and some of whom achieved national acclaim. In 1970 he eventually gave up his day job as a mechanic to take on a summer season at Pontins in Paignton, at the end of which he put together the resident trio at Harry Saltzman's River Club on the Chelsea Embankment. Saltzman was co-producer with Cubby Broccoli on the early Bond films and the producer of the Harry Palmer films; consequently the club was a popular haunt of stars of the day such as Roger Moore, Peter Sellers and Mick Jagger. Always keeping his roots in Cheltenham, Ritchie remains one of the town's very few fully professional musicians, and now works mainly as a soloist. He has a strong and loyal following in the pubs and clubs of the town and locale. (*R. Brook*)

Martin Mitchell's Fast Action, 1980. This original new wave, alternative band was originally formed in 1977 as The Rotavators, releasing the single 'Meat' on SRT Records. When the single was played on John Peel's Radio 1 programme the demand for the song was so great that it sold out the entire pressed stock of 1,000 copies in two days. Subsequently the single reached no. 15 in the alternative record charts and the band was booked to headline at the Rag Ball for the London School of Economics. With songs written and composed by Martin Mitchell and Phil Hambling, the band then went through a name change, becoming Fast Action, releasing the double A side single of 'United' and 'Dining out with Clients' on Instant Records. Once again John Peel was so taken by the band's work that he aired the single and Fast Action signed up to a record deal with Voyage International. Unfortunately that was pretty much where the fairytale ended: after recording an album's worth of material the record company went bankrupt and the bailiffs were sent in to clear their offices. Left to right: Clive Sweet, Phil Hambling, Wendy Gough, Alleyn Menzies, Martin Mitchell, John Davis. *(Alleyn Menzies)*

Performing in the Cheltenham Promenade outside what was then the general post office, *c.* 1980, are Lionel Malpas on drums, Paul Tilley on double bass, Peter May (?) on accordion, Pete Tilley on tenor saxophone. *(Anne & Jo Tilley)*

Opposite: The Premier Dance Band in the late 1980s, featuring the talents of Phil Hambling on vocals (top left), now known locally for his duo with bassist Gordon Wood, One Way Street, Alleyn Menzies (bottom left) on drums who now has his own band Al's All Stars and was a main component of local folk singer-songwriter Steve Ashley's band of the eighties, Stephen Meekums (bottom right) on bass, John Davis (top right) on guitar and Martin Fothergill (centre) on keyboards. *(Alleyn Menzies)*

The Chris Capaldi Trio. Piano and keyboard maestro and vocalist Chris Capaldi is in the centre with drummer Geoff Hawker on the left and bass player Max Sims on the right. Chris has been in the music industry for fifty years, playing keyboard with The Fortunes in the sixties and Christynash in the seventies. *(Chris Capaldi)*

Consisting of the cream of Cheltenham's jazz and funk musicians, the APO Quintet was the resident Sunday night band at Limelight during the latter part of the 1980s. Here in the atmospherically darkened basement, students were attracted in their hordes to the jazz-funk of this top band. Left to right: Mark Howells on bass has backed numerous artists such as Michael Ball, Mike d'Abo, Stephanie Lawrence and Iris Williams, and also owns Aroundabout Sound, the music shop at the far end of the Lower High Street; Paul Buck on keyboards once conducted the Count Basie Orchestra, was musical director for The Wall Street Crash, is current musical director for local big band Crescendo, is a renowned arranger and quite simply one of the country's top keyboard players; Clive Miller on drums has played for a host of big names such as Freddie Starr, Michael Ball and Stephanie Lawrence, and has taught in the town for almost twenty-five years, both at Pate's Grammar School and Bournside School; Pete Tantrum on saxophones and flute is a hugely talented musician who was once a member and featured soloist of the National Youth Jazz Orchestra, toured Scandinavia with the Mike Westbrook Orchestra, also plays locally with the Mainstreamers and is a very highly respected teacher; Midlands-based Steve Downs is on guitar. *(Clive Miller)*

THE 1990s

Pete Kearns and Tom Jurgens, Quick Swig, perform outside Cavendish House on a day which would see them perform three times at different venues around the town centre as part of the 1992 Cheltenham Fringe Festival – the other venues were in the Beechwood Shopping Arcade and in the Montpellier Courtyard. To the right of the musicians wearing sunglasses is Ian Beard, a music enthusiast who was instrumental in organising the fringe festival. *(Tom Jurgens)*

After Eight, a popular jazz trio from the early 1990s who regularly performed at Il Bottelino's restaurant in St James' Street, for £30 and a pizza! They were featured artists at the Queen's Hotel as part of the Cheltenham Literature Festival in 1993. Left to right: Martyn Court (alto saxophone), Peter Gill (piano), Mark O'Hare (guitar). *(Author)*

The hugely popular jazz funk band Pickup performing at the Axiom Centre in Winchcombe Street, *c.* 1992. Pictured are Ian Brown on trumpet, former member of The Dance Band, resident band at the Golden Valley Hotel for many years in the 1980s and 1990s and owner of Secondwind on London Road; Jonathan Boothroyd is behind Ian playing keyboards; Mark Brown at the back on bass guitar; band leader Martyn Court is on alto saxophone; Andrew McKenzie is on guitar; and just visible Paul Barker on drums. *(Martyn Court)*

Rock 'n' roll band STATE 51 performing at the Royal Oak at Gretton, November 1993. Left to right: Richard Hughes, Mark Brown, William Bick and Peter Gill. *(Author)*

Our Man in Paris taking a break from rehearsal, *c.* 1994. This acid jazz band which performed mainly original material built up a loyal following in the town, and with a slightly different line-up to the one pictured won Cheltenham's Battle of the Bands contest in 1994. Left to right: trumpeter Kirsty Hall, bassist Mark Brown, guitarist Mark O'Hare (foreground), vocalist Ricardo Orificio, saxophonist Martyn Court, drummer Matt Brodie. *(Martyn Court)*

Opposite, top: STATE 51 playing at the Cheltenham Fringe Festival, 1996. Left to right: James Adkins (bass), Paul Newman (lead guitar), Peter Gill (keyboard), Martyn Alsop (drums and vocals), Jayne Gill (tambourine). Martyn was born in Hull where he gained some chart success with a local band China Garden; he moved to Gloucestershire and joined STATE 51 in 1993 after five years playing in bands and entertaining tourists in Portugal. He is still very much on the Cheltenham music scene, currently playing with, among others, Gravy Train and Big Monkey Chequebook. *(Author)*

Opposite, bottom: The Gordon Wood band playing outside Cavendish House as part of the Fringe Music Festival, 1997. Gordon is centre stage playing bass guitar, on lead guitar on the left is Phil Bird, barely visible on drums is Martyn Alsop and on keyboard is Peter Gill. *(Author)*

Paul Newman and Alf Stokes performing at the Roses Theatre in Tewkesbury in a STATE 51 concert, 1999. Guitarist Paul was born and raised in Cheltenham (his mother owned the Patricia Newman Dancing School) and is very much part of the musical fabric of the town. Bass player Alf lived in Cheltenham for about seven years in which time he became part of the network of musicians who find themselves working together in different bands. Alf was a member of STATE 51 for almost five years but left the band when he moved to Birmingham, where he currently plays with the Lonesome Dog Blues Band. *(Author)*

Guitarist Chris Ongers with Chris Capaldi on keyboards at the Bass House, 1999. In the 1980s Chris Capaldi went on a world tour which ended up in New Orleans, where he stayed for over a year. Since returning to Cheltenham he has shared his time between performing solo, as a duo and with his own band in both local and national venues. He still makes the occasional international trip and tours Ireland regularly. Chris is certainly regarded locally as the best boogie woogie and blues player from the town with a voice that lends itself perfectly to the genre. *(Chris Capaldi)*

The Otis Mack Band in the recording studio. The name of this band, formed by guitarist Mike Croshaw and singer Andy McTaggart, originated from a nickname that Andy picked up from fellow musicians because of his passion for performing Otis Redding songs at local jam nights. Ultimately Andy became known as Otis, and whether performing with the band or solo he is regarded as Otis Mack. Standing at the back, left to right, are Lee Hunter (bass player) and Alleyn Menzies (drummer), in front are Mike Croshaw (lead guitar), Andy McTaggart (lead singer) and Colin Gibson (keyboard). *(Andy McTaggart)*

The Ramrods at the Fleet Inn, Twyning, *c.* 1999. Left to right: Graham Stodart, Tony Holbrook, Peter Jones, Alistair Barnes-Jones and Paul Newman. The Ramrods disbanded in the early 1960s, but in 1992 Peter celebrated his fiftieth birthday with a party at which previous members were invited, including John Davies and his band, The Dance Band, who were providing the entertainment. During the evening the men plucked up courage to pick up instruments that they hadn't played for almost thirty years. Today they are still performing regularly, both locally and further afield. Original band members Peter, Graham and Tony were joined by singer Alistair and guitarist Paul Newman. *(Graham Stodart)*

THE SCENE TODAY

Singer and guitarist Tom Jurgens performs as a soloist, as a duo with Pete Kearns or with his trio around Cheltenham and in the local area. Tom has a natural affinity with folk music and is one of those few solo musicians who remain sincere to their art and rely on their own created music rather than merely accompanying backing tracks. *(Tom Jurgens)*

Bob Holland and Bex Southgate pooled their musical resources in 2002 to create Bob and Bex, a duo that covers almost every aspect of the jazz repertoire. Bob is an inventive, skilful and unique pianist whose playing interacts perfectly with the smooth, versatile vocals of Bex.
(Bob Holland)

The Mainstreamers International Jazz Ensemble, featuring the awesomely talented Pete Tantrum on saxophones and flute, was the first local band to perform at the Centaur Suite at Cheltenham Racecourse in 2004. In various different line-ups the band has been appearing regularly at venues in Gloucestershire since 1993, managed by Joe Severo. Left to right: Martin Emney (drums), Geoff Meredith (trumpet), Peter Martin (double bass), Pete Tantrum and vocalist Louise Johnson. *(Joe Severo)*

The Mainstreamers at the Churchdown Club. Left to right: Joe Severo (vocals), unknown pianist, Lee Shaw, Matt Buddery, Pete Tantrum, Geoff Hyde. As the musical director Pete Tantrum uses his vast experience and influence to great effect. Among his long list of achievements is working with the Johnny Howard Band for a season in Monte Carlo, where they backed Sammy Davis Jr at the World Music Awards. *(Joe Severo)*

Performing at Cheltenham Film Studios at Arle Court are jazz piano maestro Alex Steele and on double bass John Vickers. Cheltenham Film Studios has held a regular jazz club in the last few years, encouraging local jazz stars such as Alex as well as national and indeed international stars to perform. The Studios are on the site of the one-time home of George Dowty at Arle Court. *(Alex Steele)*

Alex Steele performing with Glaswegian guitar legend Jim Mullen. As well as regularly playing at the Film Studios, the hugely talented and respected Alex is the resident house pianist at the Everyman Late Night Jazz Club, the Late Night Club of the Cheltenham International Jazz Festival and a regular pianist at the Subtone nightclub in the Promenade, which has had a chillout piano bar on its first floor since 1999. *(Alex Steele)*

JBQ – the John Beckingham Quintet. Left to right: Paul Holder (drums and vocals), John Beckingham (keyboard and lead vocals), Andy Wood (guitar and vocals), Roger Manwaring (saxophones) and Tony Capaldi (bass and vocals). JBQ is one of the best established and most respected local bands; they have featured on Channel 4 and regularly perform around the area. In recent years JBQ was the resident band at the Cheltenham Park Hotel. (Paul Holder)

Peter Brook, son of long-time Cheltenham musician Ritchie Brook and following in his father's footsteps, is establishing himself on the town's musical scene as a gifted piano and keyboard player. He regularly performs with the Mainstreamers, among others, and features in Subtone's piano bar. *(Joe Severo)*

Bass player James Linton was born in Cheltenham in 1967, emigrated to New Zealand in 1974 where he won a choral scholarship in Christchurch and then returned to Cheltenham in 1980 when his father opened the Below Stairs seafood restaurant in the Promenade. Five years later James began to play the bass for which he is now best known, regularly working with the likes of Mike d'Abo, of Manfred Mann fame and composer of such classic pop tunes as 'Handbags and Gladrags' and 'Build Me Up Buttercup'. *(Author)*

Andy McTaggart, better known as Otis Mack, plays a solo on his blues harp in a local pub. In 2000 Andy was made redundant and decided to become a full-time professional singer. As a soloist and with his six-piece band he has been busy ever since. Andy is a regular and popular performer at the local jam nights organised by guitarist Paul Newman and held at different venues on Tuesday nights: the Wheatsheaf Inn on the Old Bath Road, the Bayshill Inn, the Swan at Coombe Hill and the Royal Oak at Hucclecote are regular venues. *(Andy McTaggart)*

Paul Newman is one of the most admired and loved of Cheltenham's working musicians. He has been a professional guitarist and teacher in the area for over thirty-five years. He has taught at many of the town's top schools, including Cheltenham College and St Edward's and has been instrumental in inspiring several generations of guitarists. As a guitarist Paul is probably one of the busiest and most in demand working in the town today. His list of credits is quite formidable, including the APO Band, the Chris Capaldi Band, STATE 51 and The Ramrods. However, perhaps it is Paul's selfless organising of jam sessions around the town on a regular weekly basis for which he should be most recognised. These jam nights give opportunities to young up-and-coming musicians to work with more established and experienced musicians in front of an enthusiastic and encouraging audience. The value of these jam nights in offering experience and a chance to raise confidence cannot be overstated, and Paul's dedication to this should not be overlooked or under-valued. *(Author)*

Saxophonist Rob Peacey has been a mainstay on the local music scene for almost forty years. Originating in the Forest of Dean as a lead guitarist and playing with such groups as the Good Goods and Peggoty's People, Rob soon showed his versatility and musicality by taking up the tenor saxophone for which today he is best known. Rob has that rare gift of being at home on virtually whichever instrument he picks up, be it the guitar, saxophone, flute or piano. An architect by trade, Rob plays simply for the pleasure of making music. He fits most bills but his talents are really suited to playing jazz. *(Author)*

Guitarist Mike Croshaw played with Stevenson's Rocket from 1975 to 1977; they released three singles on the Magnet label and appearing on *Top of the Pops* in 1975 with their song 'Alright Baby'. In 1978 Mike joined Kardz who performed extensively in this country and abroad until 1981. Mike moved to Cheltenham in 1984, formed an instrumental guitar duo with Tony Smith, played in local band Backtrack and later co-formed the Otis Mack Band with Andy McTaggart. As well as teaching guitar around the area, Mike is lead guitarist in STATE 51. *(Author)*

Talented Cheltenham singer and song-writer Anita Walsh. Anita has sung with many of the locally respected bands, including the soul and blues band Blue and the Rude Tubes, hugely popular in the late 1980s and early 1990s, and the jazz afficionados The Mainstreamers. Currently Anita tours the country with the rock 'n' roll show *Let The Good Times Roll. (Anita Walsh)*

Jazz vocalist Kirsten Winter is most commonly seen in and around Cheltenham with her duo partner, London guitarist Chris Peirce, with whom she has recorded two albums, but she also sings with the Malvern Big Band and on occasion with The Mainstreamers. Her repertoire, although basically jazz, is far more versatile and her voice has both the strength required to sing with a big band and the tenderness needed to succeed in small, intimate settings. *(Kirsten Winter)*

The Jazz Badgers in Cheltenham's Yellow Shark recording studio listening to their new album *The Sett*. Left to right: Joe Griffiths (tenor saxophone), John Martin (trombone), Tom Wakefield (keyboard), Tim Miller (drums), Richard Jones (baritone saxophone), Colin Wakefield (manager), Dave Clarke (alto saxophone). All the players in this six-piece jazz and rhythm and blues band are previous members of GYJO – the Gloucestershire Youth Jazz Orchestra. *(Tom Wakefield)*

Vince Freeman and his band at the Wychwood Festival, 2006. Vince is the front man on guitar, on keyboard is Ian Munday, barely visible behind Vince is Duncan Forrester and on bass is George Elliott. A talented singer, songwriter and guitarist, Vince Freeman is a popular musician around Cheltenham's

bars and pubs both with his band and as a solo performer, but he is also appreciated much further afield, having had a six-month residency at New York's 'Bleeker Street'. *(Vince Freeman)*

One of the town's current brightest and most exciting young, unsigned bands NJAN (an acronym for Not Just A Number) largely perform their own material. Here they are performing at a local charity fundraiser. Left to right: Tom Grant (keyboards), Tobin Osiki (lead guitar), Jon Roskilly (lead vocals and guitar), Ben Humphris (drums), Mr Kool, aka Sam Grant (bass and backing vocals). *(Sam Grant)*

Opposite, top: Harry 'The Bones' Revill. Harry moved to Cheltenham in 1965 to work as a Ministry of Defence aircraft inspector, having spent most of the Second World War working on aircraft in Malta. Pictured here at the Apple Tree in Woodmancote, near Bishops Cleeve, Harry started to play the bones when he was just sixteen years old; over seventy years later he is still playing them – known to many of the town's musicians and music lovers by the energetic accompaniment he gives to those who play in the town's pubs. Harry has a natural talent for rhythm and is one of the most loved and appreciated characters of the town's music scene. *(Harry Revill)*

Opposite, bottom: Born in 1980, Cheltenham composer Stephen Selby is one of the new generation of composers and musicians in the town. He has composed for documentaries, television series, films and orchestra and symbolises the wealth of talent in the town today. *(Stephen Selby)*

Singer, songwriter and guitarist Jordan Court for a while performed locally under the pseudonym of CYAN. He is proving to be a versatile and popular member of the current Cheltenham music scene, and is currently collaborating with another singer/songwriter Kate Emerson, a former singer in Mermaid's Kiss, under the name of Blind Truth. *(Jordan Court)*

Round The Corner, one of Cheltenham's rising acoustic bands, in 2006. Left to right: Jake Spira, Peter Siret and Rory Mitchard. Along with NJAN, Round the Corner were the first to appear at the inaugural Cheltenham Band Showcase in 2007. This showcase, which is held three times a year at the Bacon Theatre, Dean Close School, is intended to highlight and promote the best in young, local musical talent and give a focus for the whole Cheltenham music community. *(Peter Siret)*

SEVEN

THE VENUES

A poster for the penultimate Cheltenham Arts Ball, 1987. Apart from raising a lot of money for charities these balls employed local bands as well as bigger names in the entertainment industry. On this occasion the star act was The Tremeloes, but playing alongside them were the Paul Dean Show Band and the APO Quintet. (Anne & Jo Tilley)

Cheltenham Town Hall. At one time the Town Hall regularly engaged local bands and musicians to perform for dances and balls, as well as booking bigger, named stars for concerts. The Musicians' Ball was annually held for many years to raise money for the local musicians' benefit fund and the Arts Ball was another regular event that benefited local musicians. The Town Hall was also regularly booked by local orchestras and choirs both large and small to stage their own concerts. Unfortunately fewer and fewer local bands perform there and with the high hire charges made by the council, with no reduction for local associations, it is becoming more of a venue for touring tribute acts and faded pop stars of the past with limited musical appeal. *(Author)*

Pittville Pump Room in Pittville Park. Recitals and concerts are still regularly staged here by local musicians, but sadly the cost of hiring the venue is fast becoming prohibitive for many local organisations for anything other than very special occasions. *(Author)*

The Everyman Theatre in Regent Street. Originally opened on 1 October 1891 as the New Theatre and Opera House with Lily Langtry as the first star performer, the architectural highlight of the theatre has always been the main auditorium designed by Frank Matcham. Until June 1959 the theatre attracted many star names, reaching a peak during the Second World War years when many of the capital's theatres were closed. However, the theatre suffered financial losses and was forced to close in June 1959. The following May it re-opened under its present name, bought and refurbished using funds raised by local theatre enthusiasts. At this point it became a repertory theatre with its own actors, musicians and technicians. It has remained open ever since except during a £3 million refurbishment in 1983, but in the mid-1990s became a touring theatre once again, pressured by finances. The Everyman still hosts many local musicians however. The CODS perform there once a year and every month in the theatre bar Cheltenham Jazz is in residence with late-night performances. *(Author)*

The Playhouse Theatre on the Bath Road is a totally amateur theatre run by volunteers. It was once the site of the municipal swimming baths, but has now been a theatre for over sixty years. It is the home of many of Cheltenham's amateur dramatic and music groups and stages productions throughout the year. On the third Sunday of every month, in the Green Room Bar, the theatre also presents jazz, usually performed by local musicians. *(Author)*

The Bacon Theatre, Dean Close School. Completed as recently as 1991, the Bacon Theatre has quickly established itself as a theatre venue to rival both the Everyman and the Playhouse theatres and a concert venue that is superior to the town hall. With comfortable seating and sensible acoustics the theatre attracts both touring professional shows, local amateur productions and performers from every genre of music (inevitably including, unfortunately, tribute acts). The Bacon Theatre is also home to the informal and intimate Prince Michael Hall, opened in 1997, and the Tuckwell Amphitheatre, site each summer of a two-week open-air festival. *(Author)*

MUSIC AT PARK HOUSE

Sunday 27ᵗʰ August 2006

****

Tra Nguyen Piano

****

PROGRAMME

Schubert was helped by the patron age of his friends: this painting by Moritz von Schwind gives an impression of a 'Schubert evening' when they gathered to hear the composer play.

Above: Park House in Thirlestaine Road, the home of architect and co-founder of the Oriel Singers George Mathers and now the venue for 'Music at Park House'. In a period spanning almost twenty years George and his wife Yoko have staged over 250 concerts. Initially these were put on at St Stephen's Church but soon moved to their own home, where they reorganise their furniture to allow up to fifty people into their drawing room to appreciate the high quality performances that they have arranged. The performers range from local talent such as cellist Warwick Cole and pianist Yoko Arai to up and coming young musicians such as pianists Tra Nguyen and Rustem Hairutinov. *(Author)*

A typical programme for one of the recitals held at Park House in Thirlestaine Road. No admission is ever charged although donations to a charitable cause are appreciated. *(George Mathers)*

The eightieth birthday celebrations of George Mathers, one of the founders of the Oriel Singers. George stands in the centre with his wife Yoko. Second from the left is choir director and conductor Tim Morris. George left the choir in 2003 but remains an active force for live music in Cheltenham. *(George Mathers)*

The Queen's Hotel in the Promenade. The hotel has over its history engaged many of the town's local musicians and Cheltenham Jazz for a while used the venue for its promotions. Today a pianist often plays in the foyer. *(Author)*

The Subtone nightclub and bar in the Promenade originally opened as a live jazz venue in the mid-1990s. Although some of the top national names were booked, sufficient numbers of local jazz enthusiasts were hard to find; since then the club has metamorphosed into one of the town's leading nightclubs. However, live music is still a priority and passion of the owners and a pianist (the likes of Alex Steele and Peter Brook) is employed from Thursday to Saturday to entertain in the upstairs chill out room, and the club still regularly books top national and international jazz names. *(Author)*

A 1950s advertisement for the Aztec Coffee Bar. Situated on The Strand, the rather downmarket Aztec had regular live, easy listening, afternoon entertainment, usually a pianist. Over the years the town centre shops, cafés and restaurants have often offered live music for shoppers and visitors. During the late 1980s and '90s Bentleys on the Strand continued the tradition by employing a regular pianist, as did Taylors (formerly Creepers), just round the corner in Cambray Place. *(Author)*

Do you enjoy . . . .

Espresso Coffee

Pleasant Music

and a

Friendly Atmosphere

Then visit . . . .

The Aztec Coffee Bar

The Strand, Cheltenham

Open from 10.30 *a.m.*

A DELIGHTFUL

CAFÉ

THE

CADENA CORNER HOUSE

PROMENADE - CHELTENHAM

(Opposite the Fountain)

The most popular rendezvous for

MORNING COFFEE

LUNCHEON

AFTERNOON TEA

Music by the MAYFAIR TRIO every afternoon

ALSO:- **THE ORIENTAL CAFÉ**

395, High Street - Cheltenham

CADENA CAFÉS LTD.

54

A popular coffee house in Cheltenham after the Second World War was the Cadena, on the Promenade opposite Neptune's Fountain. One of the most appealing features of the café was the daily, afternoon performances of the Mayfair Trio as advertised in this 1950s advertisement. *(Author)*

The Rising Sun Hotel, Cleeve Hill, has for very many years held regular music nights, largely booking local musicians. Currently every Sunday night a solo performer or duo appears in the downstairs bar. *(Author)*

The Duke of York pub in Charlton Kings on a Tuesday night in 1997. At the time the pub was famous for the jam nights organised and run by guitarist Paul Newman. Held once a month, they attracted the best local musicians to perform with the house band. Left to right: Harry 'The Bones' Revill, Paul Newman, Alf Stokes and 'Big' Tony. (*Author*)

Opposite, bottom: The Wheatsheaf Inn on the Old Bath Road. Here in the skittle alley on the right-hand side of the main building bands would regularly play in the 1950s and '60s to a packed house; it was a particularly healthy venue for the jazzers of that time. Today the pub still nobly tries to entice locals out of their living rooms by engaging top local names to perform, but the poor attendances indicate the apathy shown by many Cheltonians towards live music. However, the jam nights held at the Wheatsheaf once a month on a Tuesday do bring good audiences, and give an excellent opportunity for all local musicians to get up, play and perform with each other. (*Author*)

Jazz at the Alstone Swimming Baths on Gloucester Road, *c.* 1958. In a small room above the baths, usually on a Monday night, jazzers would gather to listen and dance to local bands such as the Delta Jazzband (pictured). Left to right: 'Squeak' Brampton (now known as Harry Brampton), John Lewis, Tat Meager, John Keen, Pete Sumner, Warren Short. *(John Keen)*

Opposite: No. 38 Priory Street. The home of Mrs Filby and her family would attain legendary status during a halcyon ten-year period. There are few who enjoyed their teenage years in the town in the 1950s and '60s who were not aware of the Filbys' home and in particular the oak-panelled basement. Between 1955 and 1965 Mrs Filby threw open the door of her home to the young people of the town and in due course it would become the centre of Cheltenham's jazz scene. Local jazz players such as Johnny Brampton, John Picton, Paul Pignon, John Keen, Mac White and Martin Fry (the last two of whom would go on to play in the Temperance Seven), to name but a few, came of age playing for the young jazzers in this basement. The young Brian Jones was a regular and stars such as Tommy Steele, Lonnie Donegan, Acker Bilk and Terry Lightfoot would often drop in after they had performed at the Town Hall. *(Jane Filby Johnson)*

The basement of 38 Priory Street, with its oak panels and full size billiard table. On most Saturday, Sunday, Monday and Thursday evenings for a decade this room would be full of the youth of the town enjoying a jazz or skiffle session. *(Jane Filby Johnson)*

The basement of 38 Priory Street, with the first Basement Jazz Band, John Picton on trumpet, *c*. 1955. The basement was originally offered to the young lads as a place in which they could rehearse. Very soon it became a place of parties and socialising for the town's jazzers and jivers. Pictured with John Picton are Harry 'Squeak' Brampton on piano, Larry Lewis on clarinet and Graham Keen on drums. *(John Keen)*

Above: Regulars of 38 Priory Street, musicians and friends. Left to right : -?-, Jill Nile (Bailey), Tat Meager, Sue Warren (Holdsworth), Adrian Montague-Smith and Jane Filby. *(Jane Filby Johnson)*

Mrs N.E. Filby looking out of 38 Priory Street. It is difficult to overstate the influence this modest lady had over a generation of Cheltenham's youth. Her home and the parties held there were respected and respectful with no alcohol and no fighting. It was a place for people to meet (many couples met there and subsequently married) and a place to enjoy jazz. She gave budding jazz musicians the chance to play in public and hone their skills. Many went on to greater musical pastures and are still playing today, but all have a common debt of gratitude.
(Jane Filby Johnson)

Mrs Filby with her son Guy on the left and John Appleby, who wrote the much sought after book *38 Priory Street and all that jazz*. When she died in 1988 the *Gloucestershire Echo* featured the loss on its front page, such was her recognised influence. *(Jane Filby Johnson)*

APPENDICES

Musicians of whatever ability, age and inclination should always be encouraged. If this book has inspired you to get involved with one of the societies that Cheltenham has to offer, learn to play an instrument or get out to listen to more live music then the following websites and telephone numbers will be of some assistance to you.

CHOIRS AND ORCHESTRAS

Charlton Kings Choral Society: www.cksconline.org.uk
Cheltenham Chamber Orchestra:
http://beehive.thisisgloucestershire.co.uk/cheltenhamchamberorchestra
Cheltenham Operatica and Dramatic Society: www.cods.org.uk
Cheltenham Philharmonic Orchestra: www.cheltenhamphilharmonic.org
Cheltenham Silver Band: www.cheltenhamband.co.uk
Cheltenham Symphony Orchestra: www.cheltenhamsymphonyorchestra.info
Cleeve Chorale: www.cleevechorale.co.uk
Cotswold Male Voice Choir: www.cotswoldmvc.org
Cotswold Savoyards: www.cotswoldsavoyards.com
Gotherington Singers: www.gotheringtonsingers.co.uk
Jubilate Chamber Choir: www.jubilatechamberchoir.co.uk
Musica Vera: http://beehive.thisisgloucestershire.co.uk/musicavera
Oriel Singers: www.orielsingers.org.uk

MUSIC TEACHERS

Paul Arthurs – Drums & Percussion – Tel: 01242 222704
Matthew Bucher – Drums – Tel: 01242 602532
Geoff Bowles – Saxophone/Clarinet – Tel: 01242 236482
Ritchie Brookes – Piano – Tel: 01242 234792

Heather Charlesworth – The Music Club of Cheltenham (Children's music workshops) – Tel: 01242 604114
Mike Croshaw – Guitar – Tel: 01242 673942
Dorothy Frances – Voice – Tel: 01242 701028
Tessa Frye – Saxophone – Tel: 01242 518302
Peter Gill – Piano – Tel: 01242 237937
Jennie Henley – Flute – Tel: 01242 700556
Bob Holland – Piano – Tel: 01242 820300
Paul Newman – Guitar – Tel: 01242 692205
Helen Wilson – Cello & Voice – Tel: 01242 699941
John Wright – Piano & Organ – Tel: 01242 251483
Helen Wright – Voice – Tel: 01242 251483

CHELTENHAM'S MUSICAL INSTRUMENT SHOPS

Aroundabout Sound – 448 High Street. Tel: 01242 578383
Cheltenham Soundhouse – 295a High Street. Tel: 01242 525967
Millennium Music – 26 Winchcombe Street. Tel: 01242 235043
Musical Instruments – 52 Winchcombe Street. Tel: 01242 517635
Secondwind – 217 London Road. Tel: 01242 584256
Vintage Strings – 88 London Road. Tel: 01242 515949

OTHER WEBSITES

Alex Steele: www.alexsteele.co.uk
Anita Walsh: www.anitawalsh.co.uk
Bacon Theatre: www.bacontheatre.co.uk
Bob and Bex: www.bobandbex.co.uk
Cheltenham Festivals: www.cheltenhamfestivals.com
Cheltenham Jazz: www.cheltenhamjazz.co.uk
Cheltenham Music Society: www.cheltmusicsoc.co.uk
Decameron: www.decameron-uk.com
Everyman Theatre: www.everymantheatre.org.uk
Felicity Lott: www.felicitylott.de
Holst Birthplace Museum: www.holstmuseum.org.uk

Jazz Badgers: www.jazzbadgers.com

Killing Joke: www.killingjoke.com

Kirsten Winter: www.kirstenwinter.com

Lonesome Dog Blues Band: www.lonesomedogbluesband.co.uk

NJAN: www.njan.co.uk

Otis Mack Band: www.otis-mack.co.uk

Peter Gill: www.petegill.com

Playhouse Theatre: www.playhousecheltenham.org

Stephen Selby: www.stephenselby.co.uk

Top Drawer: www.top-drawer.net

Vince Freeman: www.vincefreeman.com

Wheatsheaf Inn: www.wheatsheafleckhamptom.co.uk

Wychwood Festival: www.wychwoodfestival.com

Acknowledgements

In compiling any book of this nature the author is always totally reliant on the goodwill and assistance of many. I am always humbled by the generosity of friends, acquaintances and strangers who so freely give me their time and lend me their cherished and often irreplaceable photographs and memoirs. I am indebted to each and everyone of them – thank you!

In particular I would like to thank my parents for their total support, Graeme for being there, Alleyn for his tenacity, Jane Filby Johnson for allowing me to spend time with her memories, John Keen for coming up with more and more material and the following:

Mr Steven Allsup • Mr Don Baker • Mr William Bell • Mrs M Berry
Mr. Ritchie Brook • Mr Leslie Burgess • Mr & Mrs John Button • Mr Dik Cadbury
Mr Chris Capaldi • Mr Jordan Court • Mr Martyn Court • Mr Simon Fletcher
Mrs Dorothy Frances • Mr Vince Freeman • Mr Stephen Grant
Mr Robert Holland • Mrs Anne Hookey • Mr Steven Hutt • Mr David Johnson
Mr Tom Jurgens • Mr Peter Lee • Mrs Ann Maltby • Mr George Mathers
Mr Andy McTaggart • Mr Clive Miller • Mr Martin Mitchell
Miss Catherine Newbury • Mr Paul Newman • Mrs Vivian Nicholson
Mr David Palmer • Mr Robert Peacey • Mr Harry Revill • Mr David Reynolds
Mr Paul Scott • Mr Stephen Selby • Mr Joe Severo • Mr Peter Siret
Mr Frank Smith • Mr Graham Stodart • Mrs Anne Tilley • Mrs Jo Tilley
Mr Gerald Towell • Mrs Angela Walker • Miss Anita Walsh • Mr Tom Wakefield
Mr Tony Whelpton • Miss Kirsten Winter • Mr John Wright

To any that I haven't named, my apologies, but still my thanks.

Opposite: The Famous Capaldi Brothers, *c.* 1920. Carmino is on the left and Ricardo on the right. Aged just 16 in 1918, Carmino emigrated to England from Monte Cassino in Italy with his brother to join their parents, who had started up a new life in Gloucester. Struggling with a new language which they could neither speak nor write properly, the boys first of all worked with their parents selling ice cream. Soon, however, they forged a different career for themselves and in so doing started a significant musical dynasty. As accordionists Carmino and Ricardo they gained fame and popularity touring the country's theatres working alongside such names as Gracie Fields, Jimmy Jewel, Flanagan and Allen and The Crazy Gang. They also made frequent recordings on the BBC. It was Carmino's side of the family that is now best associated with Cheltenham: his son Chris and grandson Tony are firmly established in the town's musical community. *(Chris Capaldi)*

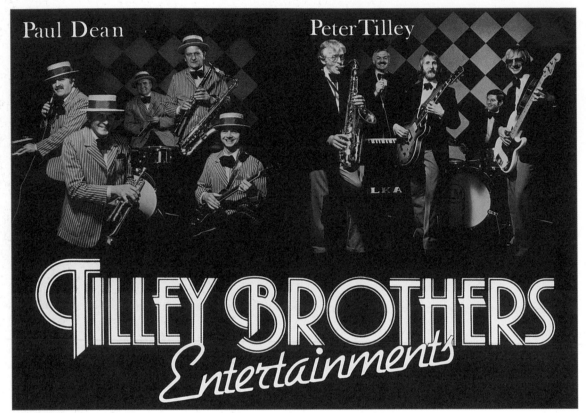

Tilley Brothers Entertainments Agency encompassed two bands: here they are. The Paul Dean trad jazz band was led by Paul Tilley and the Peter Tilley Band by his brother. Left to right in the Paul Dean Band: Peter May, Paul Tilley, Ron Dyke, Ron West (who worked with Ronnie Scott) and Tom Jame. In the Peter Tilley Band, left to right: Peter Tilley, Phil Robinson, Bob Holland, Lionel Malpas and John Bates. (Anne & Jo Tilley)